The French Way
With Vegetables

Illustrated by Oliver Caldecott

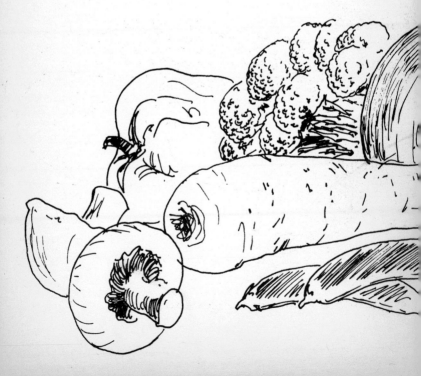

Contents

Acknowledgements		10
Introduction		11
Artichokes	Artichokes with French Dressing	13
	Stuffed Artichokes	14
	Artichokes in Cream Sauce	14
	Artichokes with Peas and Lettuce	15
	Artichoke Stew	16
	Artichoke Gratin	16
Asparagus	Asparagus Salad	18
	Baked Asparagus	19
	Asparagus in Cream Sauce	19
	Asparagus Touraine-Style	20
	Asparagus Soup	21
Aubergines	Aubergine Charlotte	22
	Aubergine Stew	23
	Baked Aubergines	24
	Aubergines with Cream Sauce	25
	Aubergine Fritters	25
	Aubergines Midi-Style	26
	Aubergines Provence-Style	27
Beetroot	Beetroot Salad	28
	Beetroot and Mint Salad	29
	Creamed Beetroot	29
	Beetroot with Onions	30
Broad Beans	Broad Bean Soup	31
	Broad Beans with Onions	31
	Creamed Broad Beans	32
	Broad Beans with Lettuce	32
	Broad Beans Touraine-Style	33
	Broad Bean Stew	34

Broccoli	Broccoli and Vegetable Stew	35
	Broccoli and Potatoes	36
	Broccoli with Butter Sauce	36
Brussels Sprouts	Brussels Sprouts Purée	37
	Brussels Sprouts Gratin	38
Cabbage	Cabbage Lorraine-Style	39
	Stuffed Cabbage Leaves	40
	Braised Cabbage	40
	Braised Red Cabbage	41
	Cabbage Loaf	42
	Red Cabbage Salad	43
	Cabbage Purée	43
	Red Cabbage with Chestnuts	44
Carrots	Carrot Soufflé	45
	Carrot Soup	46
	Carrot Purée	46
	Carrots with Spring Onions	47
	Glazed Carrots	47
	Carrots Provence-Style	48
Cauliflower	Cauliflower Fritters	49
	Cauliflower Salad	50
	Cauliflower with Egg and Breadcrumbs	50
	Cauliflower with Cheese Sauce	51
	Baked Cauliflower	52
Celeriac	Celeriac Salad	53
	Celeriac Purée	54
	Celeriac Fritters	54
	Celeriac Patties	55
Celery	Celery Salad	56
	Celery Soup	56
	Celery with Herbs	57
	Celery with Chestnuts	58
	Celery with Tomatoes	58
	Braised Celery	59
Chestnuts	Braised Chestnuts	60
Chick Peas	Chick Peas with Tomatoes	61
	Chick Pea Salad	62
	Chick Pea and Spinach Bake	62
Chicory	Chicory Salad	64

	Braised Chicory	65
	Chicory with Cream Sauce	65
	Chicory Gratin	66
Courgettes	Baked Courgettes	67
	Pickled Courgettes	68
	Courgette Flan	68
	Fried Courgettes	70
	Stewed Courgettes	70
	Courgettes with Onions	71
	Courgettes with Cream Sauce	71
	Courgette Gratin	72
Cucumber	Cucumber Salad	73
	Cucumber with Cream Sauce	73
	Cucumber Summer Soup	74
	Cucumber with Herbs	74
Fennel	Fennel Provence-Style	75
	Fennel Salad	76
	Pickled Fennel Salad	76
	Fennel Soup	77
	Braised Fennel	77
French Beans	French Bean Salad	78
	French Beans with Garlic	78
	French Beans with Turnips	79
	French Beans with Mushrooms	80
	French Beans with Tomatoes	80
	French Bean Gratin	81
Garlic	Garlic Soup	82
	Garlic and Walnut Dip	83
	Garlic Mayonnaise	83
Haricot Beans	Haricot Bean Salad	84
	Haricot Bean Soup	84
	Haricot Bean Gratin	85
	Haricot Beans Poitou-Style	86
	Southern Bean Stew	86
	Haricot Beans with Basil and Garlic	87
Herbs	Herb Salad	89
	Herb Soup	90
	Basil and Garlic Soup	90
	Basil and Tomato with Scrambled Eggs	92
	Chervil and Scrambled Eggs	92

	Dandelion and Egg Salad	93
	Dandelion with Cheese and Walnuts	94
	Sorrel Soup	94
	Braised Sorrel	95
	Sorrel Omelette	95
	Sorrel with Cream Sauce	96
	Watercress with Cream	96
	Watercress Soup	97
Leeks	Leek and Potato Soup	98
	Leek and Vegetable Soup	99
	Leek Purée	99
	Leeks and Mushrooms with Cream Sauce	100
	Leeks Savoy-Style	101
Lentils	Lentils with Mustard Sauce	102
	Lentil Purée	103
	Lentils with Spinach	103
Lettuce	Lettuce and Cheese Salad	105
	Braised Lettuce	105
	Lettuce with Mushrooms	106
	Buckwheat Pancakes with Lettuce and Cheese Sauce	107
Marrow	Marrow Provence-Style	108
	Baked Marrow	109
Mushrooms	Mushroom Omelette	110
	Mushrooms Provence-Style	111
	Mushrooms with Cream Sauce	111
	Mushroom Pancakes	112
	Mushrooms with Peppers	113
	Stewed Mushrooms	114
	Mushroom and Walnut Salad	114
Onions	Onion Soup	115
	Onion Flan	116
	Onion Fritters	117
	Onions in Sweet and Sour Sauce	117
	Onion Gratin	118
	Onion Omelette	119
	Stewed Onions	119
Parsnips	Parsnip Patties	120
	Parsnip Loaf	121

Peas	Pea Soup	122
	Peas with Lettuce and Cream Sauce	122
	Peas with Onions	123
	Peasant's Peas	124
Peppers	Pepper and Tomato Omelette	125
	Pepper and Rice Salad	126
	Peppers and Scrambled Egg	126
	Baked Peppers	127
Potatoes	Potato and Bean Salad	128
	Potato and Cream Pie	129
	Potato Soup	130
	Potato Omelette	130
	Potatoes Midi-Style	131
	Potato Gratin	132
	Potato and Cheese Cake	132
	Potatoes with Herbs	133
Pumpkin	Pumpkin Soufflé	134
	Pumpkin Pancakes	135
	Pumpkin Gratin	135
	Pumpkin Soup	136
Salsify	Vegetable Terrine with Salsify	137
Spinach	Baked Spinach	139
	Spinach Soufflé	140
	Spinach Patties	141
	Spinach Gratin	141
	Spinach with Poached Eggs	142
	Spinach with Cream	143
Sweetcorn	Grilled Sweetcorn with Tarragon Butter	144
	Sweetcorn Salad	145
Swiss Chard	Swiss Chard with Butter Sauce	146
	Swiss Chard with Eggs	147
	Swiss Chard and Apple Pie	148
	Swiss Chard Gratin	149
Tomatoes	Tomato and Vegetable Soup	150
	Tomato Salad	151
	Tomato Soup	151
	Stuffed Tomatoes	152
	Fried Tomatoes	152
	Tomatoes with Mushrooms	153

	Tomato and Courgette Summer Soup	154
Turnips	Turnips with Cream Sauce	155
	Turnip Stew	156
	Turnip Gratin	156
	Turnips with Herbs	157
	Glazed Turnips	157
Glossary		158

Acknowledgements

I would like to thank many French friends for their hospitality during my stays in France, especially Sally Guéret; also the Vegetarian Society for their help. I am grateful to those who have freely given their constructive criticism and suggestions during the compilation of the book and to my editor, Oliver Caldecott, for his continuing moral support.

Introduction

France is a large, fertile country with a variety of climates and soils, from the cool temperate north with its lush woods and pastures to the hot Mediterranean south with its olive groves and mountain slopes covered with aromatic herbs. These factors have had a profound effect on a cuisine which is distinctly regional in flavour and at the same time internationally recognizable as French.

In the countryside the approach to vegetables is simple and direct and they are generally an accompaniment to meat, game or fish. However, many of the classic vegetable soups and casseroles may form the basis of a meal in their own right. French cooks like to buy their vegetables as fresh as possible, on the day they are to be used. Always choose the best quality to get the best results. Vegetables should be bright and firm with no hint of limpness or dullness of colour. It is their fresh aroma which gives their wholesome taste so that they need to be chosen carefully. Like wine, the taste and bouquet are related to the quality.

Though French cuisine is one of the most sophisticated in the world, like all great cuisines, its origins spring from the robust cookery of the farm and country home. This classic repertoire, known as *cuisine ancienne traditionelle*, has been the inspirational base for the great creative chefs. The French are proud of this tradition for it has allowed and encouraged a vigorous cuisine which can evolve and grow.

For many centuries cooking techniques were influenced by the wood- or coal-burning range. Then, as the modern cooker became more refined, people moved away from the farms and villages to live in larger towns and cities. With this movement came a demand for new and faster cooking techniques. Since the Second World War, France has steadily grown more affluent and this has become evident in an important new

11

development which has come about in the last fifteen years. Like important movements in painting, this development sought and found a fresh approach to the preparation and presentation of food, now known as *Nouvelle Cuisine*.

Here, the accent is not only on new ingredients and combinations, but also on form and colour. A principle dedication is to a 'lyrical lightness' and a regard for the uniqueness of each ingredient. The final serving has drawn much inspiration from Japan with arresting elements of pattern and stillness, bringing a new sense of delight to the table. Nouvelle Cuisine also demonstrates a new attitude to vegetables. Their form, colour and texture are given an equal place with the other main ingredients.

Building on the discoveries of Nouvelle Cuisine, Michel Guérard's *Cuisine Minceur* (1977) answered the modern need to reduce the calorie content of French food. The reduction of cream and butter is combined with smaller portions, shorter cooking times for vegetables and a greater use of raw food (*crudités*). Since then, he and other chefs have created another facet of the new cuisine which Guérard calls *Cuisine Gourmande*. This seeks to blend the richness of the classic tradition with contemporary innovations. Whatever opinions may be, any renaissance in the world of cookery brings with it the beneficial elements of controversy, discussion and experiment. It is therefore an exciting time in which to investigate the French way with vegetables.

Naturally, the advent of the new techniques has generated criticism. Among the many positive benefits, however, is that French people are looking with new eyes at the traditional base of their contemporary cookery. This book presents a view of this tradition, as it concerns vegetables, along with some of the new developments. Be prepared to use whatever is to hand, to vary ingredients and to be experimental, for this is how the cooks of France came to create and continue to create their unique style.

Artichokes

The artichoke was brought to France from Sicily by Catherine de Medici and has been cultivated there since the sixteenth century. The main areas of cultivation today are the west of Brittany, Anjou, Provence, the valley of the Garonne, Paris and Roussillon in the south. Especially prized are the large green artichoke of Laon, the *camus* of Brittany and the violet and green of Provence. Artichokes are considered to be at their most delicious when eaten raw, while young and tender *à la croque-au-sel*, with nothing but a pinch of salt.

Artichokes with French Dressing   Serves 4
(*Artichauts à la Vinaigrette*)

4 large *or* 8 small artichokes
6 tablespoons olive oil
2 tablespoons wine vinegar
salt
freshly ground black pepper
$\frac{1}{2}$ teaspoon French mustard
1 teaspoon chopped fresh herbs

Cut off any stem of the artichokes and pull off any hard outer leaves. Cut across the top and scoop out the hairy 'choke'. Cut off any remaining sharp tips to any leaves. Put in a steamer and cook until the artichokes are just tender (30–45 minutes).

Meanwhile prepare the dressing. Whisk together the rest of the ingredients. The proportions may be varied to suit individual taste but the dressing should not be too sharp. Crushed or finely chopped garlic could be substituted for the herbs. Cool the cooked artichokes under cold water and place on a serving dish. Put a little of the dressing in the centre of each artichoke. Serve chilled or at room temperature.

13

Stuffed Artichokes (*Artichauts Farcis*)   Serves 4

4 large artichokes
juice of 1 lemon
2 tablespoons melted butter
2 tablespoons sliced button mushrooms
2 garlic cloves, finely chopped *or* crushed
3 tablespoons fresh wholemeal breadcrumbs
3 tablespoons chopped parsley
2 tablespoons olive oil
salt
freshly ground black pepper

Cut off any stem of the artichokes and pull off the hard outer leaves. Cut across the top and scoop out the hairy 'choke'. This is the cavity that will be stuffed. Cut off any remaining sharp tips to any leaves. Put the prepared artichokes in a bowl of cold water and lemon juice.

Heat the butter in a heavy pan and gently fry the mushrooms for two minutes. Add the rest of the ingredients and fry together for three or more minutes. Remove the artichokes from the lemon water and drain. Put a portion of the stuffing in each artichoke. Arrange them in a pan which can just hold them in one layer. Pour in water to just cover the bottom of the artichokes. Cover and cook over a gentle heat or steamer until the artichokes are just tender (30–45 minutes). Serve hot or cold.

These stuffed artichokes may also be baked in a medium oven until tender. Sprinkle with a little more oil before baking and bake in an ovenproof dish for about one hour.

Artichokes in Cream Sauce   Serves 4
(*Artichauts à la Crème*)

4 large artichokes
lemon juice
3 tablespoons melted butter
2 tablespoons wholemeal flour
5 fl oz (150 ml) plain yogurt
5 fl oz (150 ml) thick cream
salt

freshly ground black *or* white pepper
1 tablespoon chopped parsley

Prepare the artichokes as in the previous recipe and cut each one in quarters. Sprinkle with a little lemon juice. Heat 2 tablespoons of butter in a heavy pan and add the artichokes. Turn them gently in the butter then cover with water and cook until the artichoke pieces are tender. Remove from the heat and keep warm. Heat the rest of the butter in another pan and stir in the flour. When it just begins to turn colour, stir in the yogurt, then the cream. Add salt and pepper to taste. Add any juice in the artichoke pan and cook the sauce together until it thickens. Put in the artichokes to allow them to warm through. Pour onto a serving dish and serve garnished with the parsley.

Artichokes with Peas and Lettuce   Serves 6
(*Artichauts Clamart*)

In the days of the monarchy the *petits pois* supplied to the homes of noble Parisians came from the market gardens at Clamart. If the peas and lettuce are replaced by the same quantity of young carrots you have the dish *Artichauts Crécy* which takes its name from the town of Crécy in Seine-et-Marne where high quality carrots are grown.

12 small young artichokes
3 oz (85 g) butter
8 oz (225 g) peas
2 lettuce hearts, shredded
salt
freshly ground black *or* white pepper
1 teaspoon soft brown sugar

Prepare the artichokes as in the previous recipes. Heat the butter in a heavy pan and turn in the melted butter. Add the peas and lettuce. Season with salt and pepper to taste and add the sugar. Sprinkle with 3–4 tablespoons of water. Cover and cook on a gentle heat until the artichokes are tender (15–30 minutes). Serve basted with melted butter, adding more at the end if necessary.

Artichoke Stew (*Ragoût d'Artichauts*)   Serves 6

6 large *or* 12 small young artichokes
lemon juice
2 tablespoons melted butter
2 tablespoons olive oil
1 onion, chopped
3 large tomatoes, chopped
1 teaspoon chopped marjoram
1 teaspoon chopped basil
2 teaspoons chopped parsley
salt
freshly ground black pepper
1 pint (570 ml) vegetable stock

Prepare the artichokes as in the previous recipes. Cut each artichoke in quarters and sprinkle with lemon juice. Heat the butter and oil in a heavy pan and add the onions. Cook on a gentle heat until the onions begin to turn golden. Add the artichokes, tomatoes and herbs and turn in the oil. Sprinkle with the herbs and season with salt and pepper to taste. Stir in the stock and stew the dish gently until the artichokes are tender. Turn out onto a serving dish or serve straight from the pot.

Artichoke Gratin (*Gratin d'Artichauts*)   Serves 4

4 large artichokes
lemon juice
7 tablespoons olive oil
1 onion, chopped
3 cloves garlic, finely chopped
1 tablespoon chopped parsley
1 teaspoon chopped marjoram
1 teaspoon chopped basil
4 oz (110 g) wholemeal breadcrumbs
salt
freshly ground black pepper
2–3 tablespoons grated parmesan cheese

Prepare the artichokes as in the previous recipes. Put in a bowl and sprinkle with lemon juice. Preheat the oven to gas mark 6, 400°F (200°C). Smear an ovenproof dish with 1 tablespoon of oil. Mix together the onion, garlic, herbs, breadcrumbs with salt and pepper to taste. Stir in 4 tablespoons of oil. Put half of the breadcrumb mixture in the greased dish. Drain the artichokes and cut each one into quarters. Put the artichoke pieces on the breadcrumb layer. Cover with the rest of the breadcrumb mixture. Sprinkle with the cheese. Dribble the rest of the oil over the surface and bake in the oven for 15 minutes. Turn down the heat to gas mark 5, 375°F (190°C) and continue baking until the top is crisp and golden (about 1 hour).

Asparagus

A member of the lily family, asparagus grows wild over large parts of France, especially on poor or sandy soils. It became popular during the reign of the Sun King, Louis XIV, and has remained so in spite of its high price.

Asparagus Salad (*Salade d'Asperges*)   Serves 4

Asparagus is a delicious vegetable to eat on its own with just a little melted butter. Here, this simplicity is incorporated into a plain salad.

2 lb (900 g) asparagus
salt
1 small crisp lettuce, shredded
4 spring onions, thinly sliced
2 sticks celery
2 tablespoons chopped cucumber
2 tablespoons chopped parsley *or* watercress
2 teaspoons chopped herbs
4 oz (110 g) butter

Clean the asparagus stalks and trim to about 8–9 inches (20–23 cm) in length. Put in a steamer and sprinkle with a little salt. You may find it easier to handle the cooked asparagus if the stalks are tied in small bundles with thick thread or string. Steam until the stalks are tender (8–12 minutes).

Meanwhile prepare the rest of the salad. Mix together the salad ingredients and put in the centre of a serving dish. Melt the butter in a heavy saucepan and pour over the asparagus. Arrange the stalks around the edge of the dish. Do not make up a dressing but supply olive oil, wine vinegar, salt and fresh pepper so that the dressing can be made up to taste.

Baked Asparagus (*Asperges au Four*) Serves 4

1 lb (450 g) asparagus
salt
2 tablespoons olive oil
2 tablespoons butter
1 onion, chopped
3 large tomatoes, sliced
2 courgettes, trimmed and sliced
2 cloves garlic, finely chopped
1 teaspoon chopped oregano
1 teaspoon chopped parsley
freshly ground black pepper
2 tablespoons wholemeal breadcrumbs
2 tablespoons grated parmesan cheese

Prepare and steam the asparagus until it is tender as in the recipe for Asparagus Salad. Meanwhile heat the oil and butter in a heavy pan and fry the onion until it begins to turn golden. Add the tomatoes, courgettes, garlic, herbs, and salt and pepper to taste. Stir together well. Preheat the oven to gas mark 6, 400°F (200°C).

When the courgettes are tender, arrange the asparagus and tomato mixture in layers in an ovenproof dish. Mix together the breadcrumbs and cheese and sprinkle on the top of the dish. Bake in the oven until the top is golden (15–20 minutes).

Asparagus in Cream Sauce Serves 4
(*Asperges à la Crème*)

This dish needs to be prepared as near as possible to serving since reheating causes curdling.

1 lb (450 g) asparagus
salt
2 oz (60 g) butter
2 egg yolks
5 fl oz (150 ml) milk
1 teaspoon chopped parsley
1 teaspoon chopped tarragon
freshly ground white *or* black pepper
8 fl oz (225 ml) thick cream

Prepare and steam the asparagus until tender as in the recipe for Asparagus Salad. Melt the butter in a heavy pan and turn the cooked asparagus in the butter. Keep warm on one side.

Beat the egg yolks together with a fork in a heavy saucepan and add the milk, herbs and salt and pepper to taste. Gently heat until the mixture begins to bubble. Drain off any excess butter from the asparagus and add to the mixture. Add the cream and allow the mixture to become hot. Put the asparagus on a serving dish and pour over the sauce. Serve immediately.

Asparagus Touraine-Style   Serves 6
(*Asperges à la Tourangelle*)

At the heart of the château country, the Province of Touraine is known as the Garden of France. The asparagus of the region is particulary good and is featured here in the local style.

2 lb (900 g) asparagus
3 tablespoons melted butter
1 tablespoon olive oil
1 onion, sliced
2 cups vegetable stock
1 tablespoon wholemeal flour
salt
freshly ground white *or* black pepper
1 tablespoon chopped parsley
1 crisp lettuce heart, shredded

Trim the asparagus and cut into short lengths. Heat the butter and oil in a heavy pan and gently fry the onion until transparent. Add the asparagus and turn in the oil. Add a little stock to the flour in a cup and stir together until there are no lumps. Pour into the pan with the rest of the stock. Add salt and pepper to taste and the chopped parsley. Cover and cook together on a gentle heat for 10 minutes. Remove the lid and sprinkle over the lettuce. Cover and continue cooking until the asparagus is tender. Serve hot.

Asparagus Soup (*Crème d'Asperges*)   Serves 6

1 lb (450 g) asparagus
salt
1 tablespoon olive oil
1 tablespoon melted butter
1 onion, chopped
2 tablespoons wholemeal *or* potato flour
1 pint (570 ml) vegetable stock
1 pint (570 ml) milk
2 teaspoons chopped herbs
freshly ground black pepper
4 oz (110 g) thick cream *or* yogurt

Clean and trim the asparagus and cook in slightly salted water just enough to cover the stalks. Cook on a gentle heat and retain the liquid.

Meanwhile heat the oil and butter in a heavy pan and gently fry the onion until transparent. Add the flour and stir together well. Slowly add the stock then the milk. Stir in the herbs and pepper to taste and allow to simmer over a low heat.

Remove the cooked asparagus from the water and trim off the tips. Cut the rest of the stalks into short pieces and add to the soup, keeping the tips on one side. Add some of the asparagus water if the soup is too thick. Liquidize the soup, put back in the pan to reheat and add the cream. Do not allow the soup to boil. Serve garnished with the asparagus tips.

Aubergines

Aubergines have been cultivated in France since the beginning of the seventeenth century, especially in the warm south where they are an important vegetable in the southern cuisine. They are also known in France as *melongena* and *morelle*.

Aubergine Charlotte   Serves 6
(*Charlotte d'Aubergines*)

The word *charlotte* entered the English language as a culinary term in the nineteenth century and is usually thought of as a dessert. Here it is a delicious savoury dish.

2 lb (900 g) aubergines
salt
8 fl oz (225 ml) olive oil
1 onion, finely chopped
2–4 cloves garlic, finely chopped
2 lb (900 g) ripe tomatoes
freshly ground black pepper
1 teaspoon chopped basil
1 teaspoon chopped parsley
8 fl oz (225 ml) natural yogurt
8 fl oz (225 ml) vegetable stock

Wash and trim the aubergines. Cut into thick slices, sprinkle with salt and leave to drain in a colander for 30 minutes. Wash with cold water and allow to dry. Heat 2 tablespoons of oil in a frying pan and gently fry the onion until it just begins to turn golden. Add the garlic, tomatoes, salt and pepper to taste and the herbs. Cook together over a gentle heat for 20 minutes. Put one-third of the tomato mixture on one side to make a sauce.

In another pan fry the aubergine slices in the rest of the oil until golden on both sides. Add more oil if necessary. Preheat the oven to gas mark 4, 350°F (180°C).

Put a layer of aubergine slices in a 1¾-pint (1-litre) charlotte mould or pudding basin. Arrange the slices so that they also overlap around the edge of the mould. Spread with some of the tomato mixture and some of the yogurt. Continue making these layers until the aubergine slices and the yogurt are used up. Finish with a layer of aubergine slices. Cover the mould with foil and bake in the oven for 45 minutes. Allow to cool a little before upending it onto a serving dish. The charlotte should come out in one piece. Put the stock in a saucepan and add the remaining tomato mixture. Stir together over a gentle heat. Spoon the sauce around the edge of the charlotte and serve the rest with slices of the dish.

Aubergine Stew (*Ratatouille*)　　　　Serves 4

This is the classic vegetable stew from Provence. It should always feature the soft vegetables and tangy herbs from southern France.

1 medium aubergine
8 oz (225 g) courgettes, sliced
8 oz (225 g) pumpkin, cubed
4 tablespoons olive oil
2 medium onions, sliced
4 large tomatoes, chopped
2 red *or* green peppers, seeded and sliced
6–10 black olives, seeded and halved (optional)
2–4 cloves garlic, crushed *or* finely chopped
1 teaspoon chopped basil
1 teaspoon chopped thyme
½ teaspoon ground coriander seeds
pinch of ground aniseed
salt
freshly ground black pepper
1 tablespoon chopped parsley

Slice the aubergine lengthwise and cut each half into slices. Sprinkle the aubergine and courgette slices with a little water and leave to drain in a colander for 20–30 minutes. Heat 2 tablespoons of the oil in a large pan or casserole and gently fry the onions until they soften. Add the drained aubergines, courgettes, tomatoes, peppers, olives, garlic, herbs and salt and pepper to taste. Mix together well and sprinkle over the rest of the oil. Cover and simmer gently until all the vegetables are tender. Stir in the chopped parsley just before serving.

Baked Aubergines (*Aubergines au Four*) Serves 6

2 lb (900 g) aubergines
salt
4–6 tablespoons olive oil
2 lb (900 g) tomatoes, chopped
4 cloves garlic, finely chopped
freshly ground black pepper
1 teaspoon chopped thyme
1 teaspoon chopped basil
1 teaspoon chopped marjoram
4 oz (110 g) grated gruyère *or* cheddar cheese

Trim the aubergines and cut into thick slices. Sprinkle with a little salt and leave to drain in a colander. Wash with cold water and dry. Preheat the oven to gas mark 6, 400°F (200°C).

Heat the oil in a frying pan and fry the aubergine slices until they are golden on both sides. Put on one side to drain on kitchen paper. Put in the tomatoes once all the aubergine slices have been cooked and fry for 2 minutes. Add the garlic, salt and pepper to taste and herbs. Cook together for 10 minutes. Put half of the mixture into an ovenproof dish. Arrange the aubergine slices over this. Sprinkle with half of the cheese. Pour over the rest of the tomato mixture and cover with the rest of the cheese. Bake in the oven until the top is nice and golden (30–45 minutes).

Aubergines with Cream Sauce
(Aubergines à la Crème)

Serves 4

1 lb (450 g) aubergines
salt
6 tablespoons olive oil
2 cloves garlic, finely chopped
1 cup natural yogurt
1 cup thick cream
1 tablespoon chopped parsley
salt
freshly ground black pepper
1 teaspoon chopped mint

Trim the aubergines and cut into slices. Sprinkle with salt and leave in a colander to drain for 30 minutes. Wash in cold water and dry. Heat the olive oil in a heavy pan and gently fry the aubergine slices until they are golden on both sides. Allow to drain. In another pan, use a little of the hot oil to fry the garlic for 2 minutes. Add the yogurt, cream, parsley and salt and pepper to taste. Allow to heat through but do not allow the sauce to boil. Put the aubergine slices on a serving dish and pour over the sauce. Sprinkle with the chopped mint.

Aubergine Fritters (*Beignets d'Aubergines*)   Serves 4

2 oz (60 g) wholemeal flour
salt
2 teaspoons olive oil
1 egg white
1 lb (450 g) aubergines
oil for deep-frying
lemon slices
black olives
sprig of parsley

To make the batter, sift the flour and a pinch of salt together in a bowl. Make a well in the centre and pour in the oil and 3 tablespoons of tepid water. Gradually mix with the flour until a smooth creamy batter is formed, adding another 2 or 3 tablespoons of water as necessary. Leave on one side for 30 minutes. Just before the batter is required, beat the egg white well and fold into the batter. Mix well.

Meanwhile slice the aubergines, sprinkle with a little salt and allow to drain in a colander for 30 minutes. When the slices are ready heat the oil in a heavy pan. Bring the batter near. When the oil is hot, dip slices of aubergine in the batter and fry in the hot oil until golden. Allow to drain and arrange on a serving dish with slices of lemon and olives. Garnish with a sprig of parsley. Serve hot or cold.

Aubergines Midi-Style
(*Aubergines au Midi*)

Serves 4

In France, the South is known as the Midi. The warm climate and long summers are particularly conducive to growing the soft vegetables such as aubergines and courgettes.

1 lb (450 g) aubergines
1 lb (450 g) courgettes
salt
oil for frying
2 oz (60 g) butter
8 oz (225 g) mushrooms, chopped
1 onion, chopped
2 cloves garlic, finely chopped
4 tablespoons wholemeal breadcrumbs
freshly ground black pepper
1 teaspoon chopped oregano
1 teaspoon chopped thyme

Slice the aubergines and courgettes thickly and sprinkle with a little salt. Allow to drain in a colander for 30 minutes. Heat 6 tablespoons of oil in a heavy pan and fry the aubergine and courgette slices until just golden on each side, adding more oil as necessary. Keep warm on one side.

Melt the butter in another pan and gently fry the mushrooms

for 5 minutes. Remove and keep warm. Put in the onion, adding more oil if necessary and fry until just golden. Add the garlic, breadcrumbs, salt and pepper to taste and the herbs. Cook together for 5 minutes. Stir in the mushrooms. Arrange the aubergine and courgette slices on a serving dish and cover with the mushroom mixture. Serve hot.

Aubergines Provence-Style   Serves 6
(*Aubergines à la Provençale*)

2 lb (900 g) aubergines
salt
oil for frying
4 eggs, beaten
2–4 cloves garlic
1 teaspoon chopped parsley
1 teaspoon chopped thyme
freshly ground black pepper
3 oz (85 g) grated gruyère *or* cheddar cheese

Slice the aubergines, sprinkle with a little salt and leave to drain in a colander. Heat 6 tablespoons of oil in a heavy pan and fry the aubergine slices until just golden on both sides, adding more oil if necessary. Allow to drain. Preheat the oven to gas mark 6, 400°F (200°C).

Reduce the aubergines to a purée in a food blender and pour into a bowl. Stir in the eggs. Crush the garlic well and add the herbs and salt and pepper to taste. Pour the mixture into a greased ovenproof dish and bake in the oven until the eggs are set on top (about 10 minutes). Sprinkle with cheese, lower the heat to gas mark 4, 350°F (180°C) and bake until the top is golden (20–30 minutes).

Beetroot

Beetroot was first brought to France by the Romans who used the leaves as a vegetable. The root is now used both as a cooked vegetable and in salads. Clean the root and boil in fresh water until tender. Peel off the skin.

Beetroot Salad (*Salade de Betteraves*)   Serves 4

8 oz (225 g) cooked beetroot
1 tablespoon wine vinegar
salt
freshly ground black pepper
$\frac{1}{2}$ teaspoon French mustard
3 tablespoons olive oil
1–2 tablespoons chopped walnuts

Slice the beetroot or dice and put in a salad bowl. Make the vinaigrette by whisking together the vinegar, a pinch of salt and pepper and the mustard. Gradually whisk in the oil until the sauce is well blended. Mix with the beetroot. Sprinkle with the walnuts just before serving.

If a strong taste is required, allow the beetroot to stand in the vinaigrette for up to an hour without the nuts.

Beetroot and Mint Salad
(*Salade de Betteraves à la Menthe*)

Serves 4

This salad is adapted from the Roman dish which used the red leaves of beetroot with various green herbs.

8 oz (225 g) cooked beetroot, diced
1 large red eating apple, cored and chopped
4 spring onions, sliced
lemon juice
4 fl oz (110 ml) natural yogurt
1 tablespoon thick cream
1–2 tablespoons chopped fresh mint
salt
freshly ground black pepper
a few sprigs of watercress

Mix the beetroot, apple and onion together in a bowl. Sprinkle over a little lemon juice to just coat the vegetables. In a separate bowl mix together the yogurt, cream, salt and pepper to taste. Arrange the beetroot mixture on a salad dish. Make a space in the centre and pour in the yogurt and mint mixture. Garnish with sprigs of watercress. Fromage frais may be used instead of the yogurt.

Creamed Beetroot
(*Betteraves à la Crème*)

Serves 4

12 oz (350 g) cooked beetroot
2 tablespoons melted butter
4 fl oz (110 ml) natural yogurt
4 fl oz (110 ml) thick cream
2 teaspoons chopped tarragon
salt
freshly ground white or black pepper

Warm the cooked beetroot in the butter and keep warm on one side. In a heavy pan gently warm the yogurt and cream. Add the tarragon and salt and pepper to taste. Gently stir in the beetroot and butter. Warm through but do not allow the cream sauce to boil.

29

Beetroot with Onions
(*Betteraves aux Oignons*)

1 onion, finely chopped
2 tablespoons butter
1 tablespoon olive oil
8 oz (225 g) cooked beetroot, chopped
4 fl oz (110 g) natural yogurt
salt
freshly ground black pepper
2 teaspoons chopped parsley
2 teaspoons chopped chives

Put the onion in a heavy pan with the butter and oil and gently fry until the onion is transparent. Stir in the beetroot and turn in the oil. Add the yogurt and salt and pepper to taste. Warm through and serve garnished with the parsley and chives.

Broad Beans

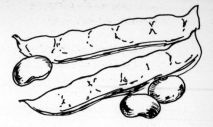

Broad Bean Soup (*Potage aux Fèves*)   Serves 6

2 tablespoons olive oil *or* melted butter
1 small bunch spring onions, chopped
1½ lb (675 g) fresh broad beans
3½ pints (2 litres) water
salt
freshly ground black pepper
2 tablespoons melted butter
2 egg yolks

Heat the oil in a heavy soup pan and gently fry the onion until transparent. Add the shelled beans and turn in the oil for 2 minutes. Add the water and salt and pepper to taste. Cook over a gentle heat until the beans are tender. Drain off the liquid and retain. Purée the beans in a food processor. Put the puréed beans and the retained liquid in the soup pan and warm through. Stir in the butter and egg yolks. Do not allow the soup to boil.

This soup is delicious with chunky bread and a little grated cheese.

Broad Beans with Onions   Serves 4
(*Fèves aux Ciboules*)

2 lb (900 g) broad beans
salt
a few sage leaves
3 tablespoons melted butter
1 bunch spring onions, chopped
1 clove garlic, crushed
freshly ground black pepper
2 teaspoons chopped savory

31

Shell the beans and cook in slightly salted water with the sage leaves until tender. Drain and retain the liquid. Keep the beans warm. In a heavy pan, heat the butter and gently fry the onions until transparent. Add the garlic, salt and pepper to taste, savory and the cooked beans. Stir together and add any of the retained liquid to make a sauce. When the garlic is well cooked serve hot.

Creamed Broad Beans
(*Fèves à la Crème*)

Serves 4

2 lb (900 g) broad beans
salt
1 teaspoon soft brown sugar
2 tablespoons natural yogurt
4 fl oz (110 g) thick cream
2 egg yolks
salt
freshly ground black pepper
1 teaspoon chopped sage
1 teaspoon chopped savory

Shell the beans and put in a pan with water to just cover. Add salt and sugar and boil until the beans are tender. Drain and retain the liquid. In a heavy pan gently heat the yogurt, cream, egg yolks, salt and pepper to taste and herbs. Stir together but do not allow to boil. Add any of the bean liquid if you want the sauce to be thinner. Put the beans on a serving dish and pour over the cream sauce.

Broad Beans with Lettuce
(*Fèves à la Laitue*)

Serves 6

2 tablespoons melted butter
1 tablespoon olive oil
1 onion, finely chopped
3 lb (1.35 kg) broad beans
2 cups water
1 teaspoon soft brown sugar
salt

freshly ground black pepper
2 teaspoons chopped sage
2 teaspoons chopped savory
$\frac{1}{2}$ crisp lettuce, shredded

Heat the butter and oil in a heavy pan and gently fry the onion until transparent. Shell the beans and add to the pan. Turn in the oil for 5 minutes. Add the water, sugar, salt and pepper to taste and the herbs. Cover and cook together for 10 minutes. Put in the lettuce and continue cooking until the beans are tender. Serve hot.

Broad Beans Touraine-Style   Serves 6
(*Fèves à la Tourangelle*)

A wine from the Loire valley will give the authentic taste to the sauce.

3 lb (1.35 kg) broad beans
2 oz (60 g) butter
a few sage leaves
2 teaspoons chopped savory
2 cups dry white wine
salt
freshly ground black pepper
2 tablespoons fromage frais *or* natural yogurt
1 tablespoon chopped chives

Shell the beans. Heat the butter in a heavy pan. Add the beans and herbs and turn in the butter for 5 minutes. Add the wine. Add salt and pepper to taste and cook together over a gentle heat for 10 minutes. Add the fromage frais and cook together until the beans are tender. Serve garnished with the chopped chives.

Broad Bean Stew (*Ragoût de Fèves*)   Serves 6

3 lb (1.35 kg) broad beans
salt
2 onions, chopped
3 tablespoons olive oil
1 tablespoon melted butter
8 oz (225 g) carrots, sliced
8 oz (225 g) young cabbage, shredded
8 oz (225 g) tomatoes, chopped
freshly ground black pepper
2 teaspoons chopped parsley
2 teaspoons chopped sage
1 cup water *or* vegetable stock
1 cup red wine

Shell the beans and boil in slightly salted water for 5 minutes.
Drain. Put the onions in a heavy pan and cook in the oil and
butter until transparent. Add the beans, carrots, cabbage,
tomatoes, salt and pepper to taste and turn in the oil. Add the
herbs, stock or water and wine and cook together until all the
vegetables are tender. Add more liquid as necessary.

Broccoli

Broccoli and Vegetable Stew
(*Ragoût de Brocolis aux Légumes*)

Serves 4

2 tablespoons melted butter
2 tablespoons olive oil
1 onion, chopped
8 oz (225 g) potatoes, chopped
1 lb (450 g) broccoli, trimmed and sliced
8 oz (225 g) courgettes, sliced
1 cup vegetable stock
1 cup wine
salt
freshly ground black pepper
2 teaspoons chopped parsley
1 teaspoon chopped tarragon
2 teaspoons chopped chives

Heat the butter and oil in a heavy pan and fry the onion until transparent. Add the potatoes and turn in the oil for 3 minutes. Add the broccoli, courgettes, stock, wine and salt and pepper to taste and cook together for 5 minutes. Add the parsley and tarragon. Cover and cook over a gentle heat until the potatoes are tender. Serve hot garnished with chopped chives.

Broccoli and Potatoes
(*Brocolis aux Pommes de Terre*)

Serves 4

2 tablespoons olive oil
1 tablespoon melted butter
1 small onion, sliced
1 lb (450 g) potatoes, par-cooked and cut in pieces
1 lb (450 g) broccoli, trimmed and cut in pieces
1 clove garlic, finely chopped
salt
freshly ground black pepper
1 cup water

Heat the oil and butter in a heavy pan and gently fry the onion until it just begins to turn golden. Add the potatoes and allow to fry a little for 5 minutes. Add the broccoli, garlic, salt and pepper to taste and water. Cover and cook together until the broccoli is tender. Test by prodding the stem with a fork. Serve hot.

Broccoli with Butter Sauce
(*Brocolis au Beurre*)

Serves 4

1½ lb (675 g) broccoli, trimmed and cut in pieces
salt
4 tablespoons melted butter
freshly ground black pepper
2 teaspoons chopped parsley

Wash the broccoli and put in a steamer. Sprinkle with a little salt and steam until the broccoli is tender. Heat the butter in a heavy pan and season with pepper and chopped parsley. When the butter is well seasoned put in the broccoli and turn well in the butter until it is well covered. Serve immediately.

Brussels Sprouts

Brussels Sprouts Purée
(*Purée de Choux de Bruxelles*)

Serves 6

Brussels sprouts may be cooked and puréed on their own. The traditional French way is to add puréed potato to the Brussels sprouts which gives the mixture more body.

2 lb (900 g) Brussels sprouts
salt
4 oz (110 g) butter
1 lb (450 g) potatoes
salt
freshly ground black pepper
pinch of freshly grated nutmeg

Trim the sprouts and cook in slightly salted boiling water until they are just tender. Heat half of the butter in a heavy pan and turn the sprouts in the melted butter. Purée the sprouts in a blender or liquidizer and keep warm.

Meanwhile cook the potatoes in a little water until they are tender. Peel. Purée in a blender and add the rest of the butter to the potatoes. Mix the puréed sprouts and potatoes together in a bowl, adding salt and pepper to taste. Serve sprinkled with a little grated nutmeg.

Other vegetables may be puréed in this simple way, such as carrot, swede or parsnip.

Brussels Sprouts Gratin

Serves 4

(*Gratin de Choux de Bruxelles*)

1 lb (450 g) Brussels sprouts
salt
2 tablespoons melted butter
4 eggs
4 fl oz (110 ml) natural yogurt *or* fromage frais
freshly ground black pepper
4 tablespoons wholemeal breadcrumbs
2 tablespoons olive oil

Preheat the oven to gas mark 6, 400°F (200°C). Trim the sprouts and boil in slightly salted water for 5 minutes. Drain and chop in a mixing bowl. Grease the bottom and sides of a gratin dish with butter.

While the sprouts are cooking, boil the eggs in water for 10 minutes. Remove the shells and chop. Add to the chopped sprouts and stir in the yoghurt, salt and pepper to taste. Put in the buttered gratin dish and cover with the breadcrumbs. Sprinkle over the olive oil and bake in the oven until the top is crisp and golden (20–30 minutes).

Cabbage

In Alsace on Maundy Thursday (Jeudi Saint) nothing but green vegetables may be eaten. Among these, the cabbage takes pride of place.

Cabbage Lorraine-Style
(*Chou à la Lorraine*)

Serves 4

This is typical of the robust mountain cooking to be found in this part of Eastern France.

1½ lb (675 g) cabbage
salt
4 tablespoons olive oil
1 onion, sliced
8 oz (225 g) tomatoes, chopped
1 tablespoon wholemeal flour
1 cup vegetable stock
½ cup wine
4 fl oz (110 ml) fromage frais *or* natural yogurt
freshly ground black pepper
1 teaspoon chopped parsley
1 teaspoon chopped marjoram

Trim the cabbage and cut into quarters. Wash in cold water and cook in slightly salted water for 5 minutes. Drain. Heat the oil in a heavy pan and gently fry the onion until transparent. Add the tomatoes and turn in the oil for 3 minutes. Add a little stock to the flour in a cup and stir together. Pour into the pan with the rest of the stock. Put in the drained cabbage and pour over the wine. Stir in the fromage frais, salt and pepper to taste and herbs. Cover and cook together until the cabbage is just tender. 39

Stuffed Cabbage Leaves
(*Feuilles de Chou Farcies*)

Serves 4

1 large Savoy cabbage
salt
1 lb (450 g) potatoes
1 onion, finely chopped
2 tablespoons melted butter
1 tablespoon olive oil
2 cloves garlic, finely chopped
4 tablespoons wholemeal breadcrumbs
2 hard-boiled eggs, chopped
1 tablespoon chopped herbs
freshly ground black pepper

Wash and trim the cabbage, discarding any damaged outer leaves. Break off up to 16 leaves and carefully place in a pan. Just cover with a little slightly salted water and boil gently until the leaves are tender. Lift them carefully from the pan and allow to drain. Meanwhile boil the potatoes in slightly salted water until tender. Peel and mash.

In another pan gently fry the onion in the butter and oil until transparent. Add the garlic and breadcrumbs and cook together for 3 minutes. Stir in the eggs, herbs and salt and pepper to taste, then the mashed potato. Mix together well.

Lay out each cabbage leaf, stem downwards and place a portion of the stuffing mixture in the centre. Fold up like an envelope. Place the cabbage envelopes in a steamer and steam for 5 minutes to warm through. Serve hot or cold.

Braised Cabbage (*Chou Braisé*)

Serves 4

1½ lb (675 g) cabbage
salt
2 tablespoons melted butter
2 tablespoons olive oil
1 onion, sliced
1½ cups vegetable stock
½ cup wine
freshly ground black pepper

Trim the cabbage and cut in quarters. Wash well in cold water and boil in slightly salted water for 5 minutes. Drain. Heat the butter and oil in a heavy pan and gently fry the onion until transparent. Add the cabbage and turn in the oil. Add the stock, wine and salt and pepper to taste. Cook together for a few more minutes until the cabbage is tender. Do not allow the cabbage to soften.

Braised Red Cabbage   Serves 4
(*Chou Rouge Braisé*)

A good Burgundy wine is an essential ingredient in this recipe from the Ardennes in northern France.

1 medium-sized red cabbage
2 tablespoons melted butter
1 tablespoon olive oil
1 onion, sliced
1 tablespoon brown sugar
1 tablespoon wine vinegar
5 fl oz (150 ml) dry red wine
salt
freshly ground black pepper

Preheat the oven to gas mark 4, 350°F (180°C). Trim the cabbage and shred finely. Heat the butter and oil in a heavy pan and stir in the onion. Fry over a gentle heat until transparent. Add the sugar and stir together until the sugar caramelizes. Add the cabbage and vinegar and stir together. Add the wine and salt and pepper to taste. Cover the pan and bake in the oven until the cabbage is tender (about 45 minutes). Remove the lid 10 minutes before the end of the cooking to allow the excess moisture to evaporate.

Cabbage Loaf (*Pain au Chou*)   Serves 6

2 lb (900 g) cabbage
salt
2 heaped tablespoons wholemeal flour
freshly ground black pepper
1 tablespoon olive oil
3 eggs
4 fl oz (110 ml) milk
freshly grated nutmeg
butter

For the white sauce (*sauce velouté*):
1 oz (30 g) butter
1 oz (30 g) wholemeal flour
15 fl oz (430 ml) milk
5 fl oz (150 ml) cream
salt
freshly ground white pepper
lemon juice

Trim the cabbage and cut into quarters. Wash in cold water. Boil in slightly salted water until the cabbage is tender. Drain and chop well. In a mixing bowl, sift together the flour, a pinch of salt and a little pepper. Stir in the olive oil. Beat the eggs and stir into the flour. Slowly stir in the milk. Cover with a damp cloth and leave to stand for 30 minutes. 10 minutes before the end of this time, preheat the oven to gas mark 6, 400°F (200°C).

Stir the chopped cabbage into the batter and sprinkle over a little grated nutmeg. Put the mixture into a well-buttered ovenproof dish and bake in the oven until the loaf is well set (30–40 minutes). Keep warm while you prepare the sauce.

Melt the butter in a heavy pan over a low heat. Stir in the flour and stir together for 2 minutes. In sauce-making, this is known as the white *roux*. Remove the roux from the heat. As soon as the roux has stopped bubbling whisk in the milk which should be very hot but not boiling. Whisk well until the sauce is well blended. You now have the sauce velouté. This is enriched to go with the cabbage loaf by beating in the cream by the spoonful. Keep the sauce simmering and add salt, pepper and lemon juice to taste. Pour over slices of the cabbage loaf.

Red Cabbage Salad
(*Salade de Chou Rouge*)

Serves 4

10 oz (285 g) red cabbage
1 tablespoon sliced onion
2 tablespoons sliced radishes
2 tablespoons chopped walnuts
1 tablespoon wine vinegar
salt
freshly ground black pepper
$\frac{1}{2}$ teaspoon French mustard
3 tablespoons olive oil

Wash the cabbage and trim. Slice finely and put into a salad bowl. Add the onions, radishes and walnuts. In a separate bowl whisk together the vinegar with a pinch of salt and pepper and the mustard. Gradually whisk in the oil. Pour the vinaigrette over the red cabbage salad. Allow to stand for 1 hour before serving.

Cabbage Purée (*Purée de Chou*)

Serves 4

2 lb (900 g) cabbage
1 onion, sliced
pinch of chopped thyme
pinch of chopped marjoram
pinch of chopped basil
2 tablespoons melted butter
2 tablespoons thick cream
salt
freshly ground black pepper
pinch of freshly grated nutmeg

Trim the cabbage and slice. Boil in a little water with the onion and herbs. When the cabbage is tender purée in a blender or liquidizer. Put into a serving bowl and stir in the butter, cream, salt and pepper to taste. Sprinkle with a little grated nutmeg. Serve with sliced apples.

Red Cabbage with Chestnuts

Serves 4

(*Chou Rouge aux Marrons*)

This dish is popular in the region of Limousin where there are still forests of chestnut trees.

8 oz (225 g) fresh chestnuts
1 lb (450 g) red cabbage
2 oz (60 g) butter
2 tablespoons red wine vinegar
1 cup vegetable stock
salt
freshly ground black pepper
1 large cooking apple, peeled, cored and chopped
1 tablespoon soft brown sugar

Make a slit in each of the chestnuts and boil in water until tender. Skin the chestnuts, allow to cool and slice. Trim the cabbage, quarter and slice. Heat the butter in a heavy pan and fry the cabbage for 3 minutes. Add the chestnuts, vinegar, stock, salt and pepper to taste, apple and sugar. Stir together and cover. Simmer over a gentle heat for 15 minutes. Serve hot.

Carrots

Carrot Soufflé (*Soufflé aux Carottes*)   Serves 4

butter
3 tablespoons grated parmesan cheese
1 lb (450 g) carrots, peeled and chopped
salt
2 tablespoons flour
½ pint (300 ml) milk
3 eggs and 1 egg white
freshly ground white pepper

Prepare the soufflé dish by smearing the inside with butter and coating with grated parmesan cheese. Tie a band of buttered greaseproof paper round the outside of the dish so that it is about 2 inches (5 cm) higher than the edge.

Cook the carrots in boiling slightly salted water until tender. Drain. Purée in a food processor or pound through a sieve. Return the purée to the pan and allow the excess moisture to evaporate over a gentle heat. Remove from the heat. Preheat the oven to gas mark 6, 400°F (200°C).

Melt 2 tablespoons of butter in another saucepan and add the flour. Stir together for 2 minutes over a gentle heat then gradually stir in the milk. Bring to the boil, stirring continuously for 7 minutes. Add the carrot purée and allow to cool. Separate the egg yolks from the whites and add the yolks to the carrot mixture. Stir in salt and pepper to taste. Whisk the 4 egg whites until stiff. Fold 1 tablespoon of egg white into the carrot mixture then carefully fold in the remaining whites in three amounts. Pour the whole mixture into the prepared soufflé dish. Cook in the oven until the soufflé rises (20–25 minutes). Serve immediately.

45

Carrot Soup (*Potage aux Carottes*)   Serves 6

2 tablespoons olive oil
1 onion, finely chopped
1 lb (450 g) carrots, chopped
10–12 oz (285–350 g) potatoes, chopped
3 pints (1.7 litres) water *or* thin vegetable stock
salt
freshly ground black pepper
1 tablespoon chopped parsley

Heat the oil in a heavy soup pan and gently fry the onion until transparent. Add the carrots and potatoes and turn in the oil for 3 minutes. Pour in the water or stock and season with salt and pepper to taste. Cover and cook until the vegetables are tender. Purée in a blender or liquidizer. Serve hot, garnished with chopped parsley.

    This soup is excellent with chunks of bread or croûtons.

Carrot Purée (*Purée de Carottes*)   Serves 6

3 lb (1.35 kg) carrots
salt
3 tablespoons melted butter
1 small onion, finely chopped
salt
freshly ground black pepper
1 teaspoon chopped tarragon
3 tablespoons thick cream

Trim the carrots and peel. Chop and boil in slightly salted water until the carrots are tender. Purée in a blender or liquidizer. Put back in the pan and add salt and pepper to taste, tarragon, melted butter and cream. Heat the purée gently but do not allow it to bubble.

Carrots with Spring Onions
(*Carottes aux Ciboules*)

Serves 4

1 lb (450 g) carrots
salt
3 tablespoons melted butter
1 bunch spring onions, chopped
8 oz (225 g) frozen peas
1 cup vegetable stock
freshly ground black pepper
a few sage leaves

Peel and trim the carrots and slice. Boil in slightly salted water until almost tender. Drain. Heat the butter in a heavy pan and gently fry the spring onions for 2 minutes. Add the carrots and peas along with the stock, salt and pepper to taste and sage leaves. Cover and cook together until the carrots are tender.

Glazed Carrots (*Carottes Glacées*)

Serves 4

8 baby carrots
1 pint (600 ml) stock *or* water
1 oz (30 g) butter
1–2 teaspoons caster *or* icing sugar
pinch of salt
freshly ground black pepper

Peel the carrots as necessary and trim off most of the green leaves. Put the carrots in a saucepan which just allows them to lie flat. Add the stock, butter, sugar and salt and pepper to taste. Allow to simmer until most of the liquid has evaporated (20 minutes), leaving the carrots glazed with a thick syrup.

Carrots Provence-Style
(*Carottes à la Provençale*)

Serves 4

3 tablespoons melted butter
3 tablespoons olive oil
1 onion, chopped
1 lb (450 g) carrots, sliced
8 oz (225 g) tomatoes, chopped
8 oz (225 g) courgettes, sliced
2–4 cloves garlic, finely chopped
6–10 olives, stoned and sliced
2 teaspoons chopped parsley
2 teaspoons chopped basil
½ cup water *or* vegetable stock
½ cup wine
salt
freshly ground black pepper

Heat the butter and oil in a heavy pan and gently fry the onion until transparent. Add the carrots, tomatoes, courgettes, garlic, olives and turn in the oil for 2 minutes. Add the herbs, stock, wine and salt and pepper to taste. Cover and simmer until the carrots are tender.

Cauliflower

Cauliflowers have been known in Italy since the sixteenth century from where they were brought to France. They should always be bought when the leaves are green since this is a freshness indicator.

Cauliflower Fritters
(Beignets de Chou-fleur)

Serves 4

1 lb (450 g) cauliflower
1 egg, beaten
1½ tablespoons wholemeal flour
pinch of baking powder
pinch of salt
pinch of freshly ground black pepper
4 tablespoons olive oil
1 tablespoon lemon juice
1 tablespoon chopped fresh herbs
oil for deep frying
1 lemon, cut into wedges

Trim the cauliflower and cut into small sprigs. Wash well in cold water and drain well. Make up the fritter batter by beating together the egg, flour, baking powder, salt and pepper with a little water to make a thin creamy consistency. Allow to stand for 30 minutes.

Meanwhile make up a marinade for the cauliflower. Mix together the olive oil, lemon juice and herbs. Turn the cauliflower sprigs in this marinade and allow to stand until the batter is ready. Heat the oil in a deep pan until it is quite hot. Put the sprigs into the batter and make sure they are well coated. Fry in the hot oil until golden. Remove with a slotted spoon and allow to drain on absorbent paper. Serve with lemon wedges.

Cauliflower Salad
(Salade de Chou-fleur)

Serves 4

1 lb (450 g) cauliflower
2 tablespoons almonds, blanched and sliced

For the mayonnaise:
2 egg yolks
2 tablespoons white wine vinegar
1 teaspoon dry *or* French mustard
salt
freshly ground white pepper
10 fl oz (285 ml) sunflower oil

2 teaspoons chopped tarragon

Trim the cauliflower and break into small sprigs. Wash well in cold water and drain. Put in a bowl and stir in the almonds.

Meanwhile make sure that all the mayonnaise ingredients are at room temperature so that they will blend properly. Beat the egg yolks in a bowl with half of the vinegar. Beat in the mustard, salt and pepper to taste until the mixture thickens. Whisk in the oil drop by drop. After 2 tablespoons of oil have been added the mixture should be quite thick. Keep adding the rest of the oil gradually. Check the seasoning, adding the rest of the vinegar if this taste is required. Serve at room temperature. 1 tablespoon of lemon juice may be substituted for the wine vinegar. Olive oil or other vegetable oil may be substituted for the sunflower oil.

Stir the mayonnaise into the cauliflower and sprinkle over the tarragon.

Cauliflower with Egg and Breadcrumbs
(Chou-fleur à la Polonaise)

Serves 4

1 good-sized cauliflower
2 oz (60 g) butter
3 tablespoons wholemeal breadcrumbs
salt
freshly ground black pepper
1 hard-boiled egg, finely chopped
1 tablespoon chopped parsley

Trim the cauliflower and cut into pieces. Wash well and cook in boiling water until just tender. Drain and put in a greased ovenproof dish. Melt the butter in a heavy pan and fry the breadcrumbs until they begin to turn golden. Mix in salt and pepper to taste and sprinkle over the cauliflower. Put under the grill for 5 minutes to heat through. Garnish with the egg and parsley. Serve hot.

Cauliflower with Cheese Sauce   Serves 4
(*Chou-fleur au Gratin*)

1 good-sized cauliflower
salt
3 tablespoons butter
1 onion, sliced
2 tablespoons wholemeal flour
6 oz (170 g) grated gruyère *or* cheddar cheese
freshly ground black pepper
½ teaspoon chopped oregano
½ teaspoon chopped marjoram
½ teaspoon dry *or* French mustard
pinch of grated nutmeg

Trim the cauliflower and cut into pieces. Wash well in cold water and drain. Boil in slightly salted water until tender. Drain and retain the liquid. Preheat the oven to gas mark 6, 400°F (200°C).

Heat the butter in a heavy pan and gently fry the onion until transparent. Gradually stir in the flour. Slowly add the cauliflower liquid and half of the grated cheese. Season with salt and pepper to taste, the herbs and mustard. Add more liquid in the form of hot water or vegetable stock to make a thick sauce. Put the cauliflower in a greased ovenproof dish and pour over the sauce. Sprinkle over the nutmeg and the rest of the cheese. Bake in the oven until the top is crisp and golden (15–25 minutes).

Baked Cauliflower
(*Pain de Chou-fleur*)

Serves 6

1 good-sized cauliflower
salt
1 quantity white velouté (see under Cabbage Loaf)
freshly ground black pepper
2 eggs, beaten
3 tomatoes, sliced
1 tablespoon chopped parsley

Trim the cauliflower and cut in pieces. Wash well in cold water and boil in slightly salted water until tender. Purée the cauliflower in a blender or liquidizer. Preheat the oven to gas mark 6, 400°F (200°C).

Make the white velouté without adding cream to it and reduce it over a gentle heat until it is quite thick. In a bowl stir together the puréed cauliflower and the thick sauce. Season with salt and pepper to taste and add the beaten eggs. Put the mixture in a greased ovenproof dish and cover with some of the sliced tomato. Bake in the oven for 30 minutes. Turn out onto a serving dish and garnish with the rest of the tomato slices and chopped parsley.

Celeriac

This plant is a variety of celery which has a large edible root. It is this part of the plant which is used and it should always be firm when purchased.

Celeriac Salad
(Salade de Céleri-rave)

Serves 4

1 lb (450 g) celeriac
salt

For the sauce:
6 oz (170 g) unsalted butter
3 egg yolks
salt
freshly ground white pepper
juice of $\frac{1}{2}$ lemon

1 tablespoon chopped capers

Peel and trim the celeriac and cut into short thin strips. Cook in boiling slightly salted water for 1 minute. Remove and drain. Meanwhile make the Hollandaise sauce.

Melt the butter over a gentle heat in a heavy pan. In another pan whisk the egg yolks and 2 tablespoons of water with a little salt and pepper to taste for half a minute. Put on a gentle heat and remove the butter. Continue whisking until the mixture is creamy and the whisk begins to leave a trail. Remove from the heat. Slowly add the melted butter to the egg mixture a few drops at a time. Once the butter has been added, check the seasoning and add lemon juice to taste. Stir in the capers and pour over the celeriac in a serving dish.

Celeriac Purée
(*Purée de Céleri-rave*)

Serves 4

1 lb (450 g) celeriac
8 oz (225 g) potatoes
salt
2 tablespoons butter
2 tablespoons thick cream
freshly ground pepper
pinch of nutmeg
1 teaspoon chopped mint

Peel and trim the celeriac and cut in pieces. Boil in water until tender. Drain. Boil the potatoes in slightly salted water until tender. Drain and peel. Put both vegetables in a blender or liquidizer and reduce to a purée. Put in a serving dish and stir in the butter, cream, salt and pepper to taste and nutmeg. Garnish with the chopped mint.

Celeriac Fritters
(*Beignets de Céleri-rave*)

Serves 4

12 oz (350 g) celeriac
salt
2 tablespoons wholemeal flour
3 tablespoons wholemeal breadcrumbs
1 egg, beaten
2 tablespoons melted butter
2 tablespoons olive oil

For the sauce:
2 oz (60 g) walnuts, chopped
3 tablespoons butter
2 tablespoons grated parmesan cheese
1 clove garlic
2 tablespoons thick cream
salt
freshly ground black pepper
vegetable stock

Peel and trim the celeriac and cut into strips as in Celeriac Salad.

Boil in slightly salted water for 10 minutes. Drain. Mix the flour with the breadcrumbs. Put the beaten egg in a bowl and put in the celeriac strips so that they are well coated with egg. Roll in the egg and breadcrumb mixture. Heat the butter and oil in a heavy frying pan and fry the celeriac strips until just golden. Keep warm.

Make the sauce by pounding the nuts, butter, cheese and garlic to make a thick paste. Stir in the cream and season with salt and pepper to taste. Put in a pan and heat gently. Gradually add stock until a sauce is made of the required consistency. Serve with the celeriac strips.

Celeriac Patties
(*Croquettes de Céleri-rave*)

Serves 4–6

1 lb (450 g) celeriac
salt
1 lb (450 g) potatoes
3 egg yolks
freshly ground black pepper
pinch of freshly grated nutmeg
1 teaspoon chopped parsley
wholemeal flour
oil for deep-frying
lemon wedges

Peel and trim the celeriac and cut into pieces. Boil in slightly salted water until tender. Drain and mash. Boil the potatoes in slightly salted water until soft. Peel and mash. Mix the celeriac and potato in a bowl with the egg yolks, seasoning and parsley. Squeeze together to make walnut-sized balls. Roll in flour and flatten slightly. Deep-fry in hot oil until golden on both sides. Serve with lemon wedges.

Celery

Although introduced by the Romans, celery was not widely cultivated in France until the sixteenth century. The Loire valley is the principal region of production. Make sure the stalks are always firm and crisp. Celery is sold in France with the leaves intact and they make an excellent flavouring herb.

Celery Salad (*Salade de Céleri*)   Serves 4

1 head of celery
juice of half lemon
mayonnaise (see recipe under Cauliflower Salad)

Wash and trim the celery. Slice and put in a bowl. Sprinkle with lemon juice and leave to stand while you prepare the mayonnaise. Check the seasonings, adding more mustard, salt and pepper if desired. Add enough of the mayonnaise to coat the celery and mix well. Cover with a cloth and leave to stand for 1 hour before serving.

Celery Soup (*Potage au Céleri*)   Serves 6

2 tablespoons melted butter
1 onion, finely chopped
8 oz (225 g) potatoes, chopped
1 lb (450 g) celery, trimmed and chopped
salt
freshly ground pepper
2½ pints (1.43 litres) warm water
1 teaspoon celery seed (optional)
2 fl oz (60 ml) thick cream

Heat the butter in a heavy soup pan and gently fry the onion until transparent. Add the potatoes and celery. Keep a little of the celery leaf as a garnish. Turn in the oil. Add salt and pepper to taste and the water and celery seed. Cook the celery and potato until both vegetables are tender. Purée in a blender or liquidizer. Put back in the pan and add the cream. Heat gently but do not allow to boil.

Celery with Herbs   Serves 4
(*Céleri en Branche aux Fines Herbes*)

2 heads of celery
salt
butter
bunch of chopped fresh tarragon
2 teaspoons chopped marjoram
$\frac{1}{2}$ cup vegetable stock
$\frac{1}{2}$ cup dry wine
freshly ground black pepper
3 tablespoons wholemeal breadcrumbs
3 tablespoons fromage frais *or* natural yogurt
1 teaspoon chopped parsley

Trim the celery and cut the stalks into large pieces. Cook in boiling slightly salted water until just tender. Drain. Put in a well-buttered ovenproof dish. Preheat the oven to gas mark 4, 350°F (180°C).

Put the tarragon and marjoram in a small heavy pan and pour over the stock and wine. Season with salt and pepper to taste and heat gently for 10 minutes. Pour over the celery. Sprinkle over the breadcrumbs and spread with the fromage frais. Bake in the oven until the top begins to turn golden (20–30 minutes). Serve sprinkled with chopped parsley.

Celery with Chestnuts
(*Céleri en Branche aux Marrons*)

Serves 4

1 head celery
lemon juice
1 lb (450 g) chestnuts
2 tablespoons melted butter
salt
freshly ground black pepper
vegetable stock

Trim the celery, cut into pieces, keep some of the green leaf to garnish. Put in a bowl and sprinkle with lemon juice. Put the chestnuts in a pan after pricking with a fork. Cover with water and boil for 10 minutes. Drain and peel. Put the butter in a heavy pan and add the peeled chestnuts. Heat gently and turn the chestnuts in the butter. Season with salt and pepper to taste and pour in enough stock to just cover. Put the lid on the pan and simmer gently for 5 minutes. Add the celery pieces. Make sure there is enough stock to just cover the chestnuts and celery, adding more if necessary. Continue simmering gently until the chestnuts are tender. Serve garnished with a little chopped celery leaf.

This dish also goes well with a white sauce. See under the recipe for Cabbage Loaf.

Celery with Tomatoes
(*Céleri aux Tomates*)

Serves 4

3 tablespoons melted butter
1 tablespoon olive oil
1 onion, finely chopped
8 oz (225 g) tomatoes, chopped
1 head celery
1 teaspoon chopped thyme
1 teaspoon chopped basil
salt
freshly ground black pepper
1 cup vegetable stock
½ cup red wine
2 teaspoons chopped parsley

Heat the butter in a heavy pan with the olive oil. Gently fry the onion until transparent. Add the tomatoes and turn in the oil. Trim the celery and cut in pieces. Add to the tomatoes with the herbs, salt and pepper to taste. Stir together and add the stock and wine. Cover and cook on a gentle heat until the celery is tender (about 5 minutes). Serve garnished with chopped parsley.

Braised Celery (*Céleri Braisé*)   *Serves 4*

2 heads celery
salt
1 onion, finely chopped
3 tablespoons melted butter
1 tablespoon olive oil
2 tablespoons wholemeal flour
1 cup vegetable stock
1 cup dry wine
freshly ground black pepper

Trim the celery and cut into pieces. Blanch in slightly salted boiling water for 2 minutes. Drain. Put the onion in a heavy pan with the butter and olive oil and gently fry until the onion just begins to turn golden. Stir in the flour and add the celery pieces. Turn well in the *roux*. Gradually add the stock and wine. Season with salt and pepper to taste. Cook together until the celery is just tender (a few minutes).

Chestnuts

Chestnuts are used in many parts of France as a vegetable, especially where they are plentiful as in the regions of Poitou and Limousin. To prepare them for cooking, make a slit in the shell with a knife and place in a pan of cold water. Bring to the boil and allow to simmer for 5 minutes. Drain and cool under cold water. Now the shell and skin can be removed with a sharp knife.

Braised Chestnuts (*Marrons Braisés*)   Serves 4–6

2 lb (900 g) chestnuts
2 sticks celery, chopped
1 teaspoon brown sugar
2 oz (60 g) butter
salt
freshly ground black pepper

Prepare the chestnuts for cooking as described above. Put in a heavy pan with the celery, sugar and butter. Season with salt and pepper. Pour on enough water to just cover. Bring to the boil and simmer together until the chestnuts are tender (about 30 minutes). Raise the heat at the end to allow the excess liquid to evaporate. Remove the celery before serving.

To make chestnut purée, cook the chestnuts in milk or stock with the rest of the ingredients. Remove the celery and purée the chestnuts in a food processor or pound through a sieve. Beat in a little more melted butter before serving.

Chick Peas

There are many varieties of this Mediterranean legume, one of which is cultivated in France. Soak dried chick peas in water the day before required. Next day change the water and boil for 10 minutes. Drain and continue boiling in fresh water until the chick peas are tender. Tinned chick peas may also be used, in which case no pre-boiling is necessary.

Chick Peas with Tomatoes
(*Pois Chiches aux Tomates*)

Serves 4

4 tablespoons olive oil
1 onion, finely chopped
1 lb (450 g) tomatoes, chopped
1 lb (450 g) cooked chick peas
2–4 cloves garlic, finely chopped
1 teaspoon chopped sage
1 teaspoon chopped basil
1 teaspoon chopped thyme
salt
freshly ground black pepper
½ cup red wine
½ cup vegetable stock
1 tablespoon chopped parsley

Heat the oil in a heavy pan and fry the onion until it just begins to turn golden. Add the tomatoes and turn in the oil for 5 minutes. Add the chick peas, garlic, herbs, salt and pepper to taste and turn in the oil. Add the wine and stock. Cover and cook together for 10 minutes. Serve garnished with chopped parsley.

Chick Pea Salad
(*Salade de Pois Chiches*)

Serves 4

1 lb (450 g) chick peas, cooked with a bay leaf and a few cloves
olive oil
wine vinegar
salt
freshly ground black pepper
sliced spring onions
chopped parsley

Arrange the chick peas in a serving dish and serve with the rest of the ingredients to taste. People can have individual servings of peas and make up their own dressings. Lemon juice may be substituted for the wine vinegar. Other herbs such as fresh tarragon may be added to the dish as desired.

Chick Pea and Spinach Bake
(*Gratin de Pois Chiches aux Épinards*)

Serves 6

2 lb (900 g) fresh spinach
salt
4 tablespoons olive oil
1 small onion, finely chopped
8 oz (225 g) tomatoes, chopped
2–4 cloves garlic, finely chopped
2 teaspoons chopped basil
1 teaspoon chopped savory
freshly ground black pepper
10 oz (285 g) cooked chick peas
2 hard-boiled eggs
a few sage leaves
3 tablespoons wholemeal breadcrumbs
2 tablespoons melted butter

Trim the spinach and boil in slightly salted water for 3 minutes. Drain and chop. Preheat the oven to gas mark 6, 400°F (200°C).

Heat the olive oil in a heavy pan and gently fry the onion until transparent. Add the tomatoes and fry together until the tomatoes soften. Add the garlic, herbs, salt and pepper to taste. Cook together for 5 minutes. Mix the chick peas with the tomatoes. Chop the eggs in a bowl and beat in the spinach and sage leaves. Stir into the tomato and chick peas and put the mixture in a greased ovenproof dish. Cover with the bread-crumbs and dribble over the melted butter. Bake in the oven until the top is crisp and golden (20–30 minutes).

Chicory

Chicory is known in Belgium as *chicorée de Bruxelles* and in the United States as endive. It is a tight-leaved vegetable with a pale centre and dark outer leaves.

Chicory Salad (*Salade d'Endives*)   Serves 6

8 oz (225 g) chicory
8 oz (225 g) red-skinned apples
4 oz (110 g) small mushrooms
6 fl oz (170 ml) natural yogurt *or* fromage frais
salt
freshly ground black pepper
handful chopped walnuts
4 oz (110 g) cooked beetroot
lemon juice

Trim the chicory and cut into thick slices. Core the apples and cut into small chunks. Slice the mushrooms. Put the chicory, apples and mushrooms into a salad bowl. In a separate bowl mix together the yogurt, salt and pepper to taste and the walnuts. Pour over the salad vegetables and mix together. Chop the beetroot into small pieces and spread over the salad. Sprinkle with lemon juice to taste.

Braised Chicory (*Endives Braisées*)   Serves 4

1½ lb (675 g) chicory
2 tablespoons melted butter
salt
freshly ground black pepper
1 teaspoon soft brown sugar
1 tablespoon lemon juice
1 tablespoon chopped parsley

Preheat the oven to gas mark 4, 350°F (180°C). Trim the chicory heads. Spread the bottom and sides of an oven-proof dish with butter. Put in the chicory. Sprinkle with salt, pepper, sugar, lemon juice and 2 tablespoons of water. Cover the dish with a piece of foil and bake in the oven until the chicory heads are tender inside (50–60 minutes). Serve garnished with the chopped parsley.

Chicory with Cream Sauce   Serves 4
(*Endives à la Crème*)

1½ lb (675 g) chicory
2 tablespoons melted butter
salt
freshly ground black pepper
1 teaspoon soft brown sugar
1 tablespoon lemon juice
1 cup thick cream
½ cup vegetable stock
2 tablespoons dry white wine
lemon slices
2 teaspoons chopped parsley

Prepare the chicory as in the previous recipe for Braised Chicory. Meanwhile gently heat the cream, stock and wine together in a heavy pan. Do not allow to boil. Season with salt and pepper to taste. When the chicory is cooked pour over the cream sauce and serve garnished with lemon slices and chopped parsley.

Chicory Gratin (*Endives au Gratin*)   Serves 4

1½ lb (675 g) chicory
butter
salt
freshly ground black pepper
3 tablespoons grated parmesan cheese
3 tablespoons wholemeal breadcrumbs
1 tablespoon chopped parsley
2 tablespoons olive oil *or* melted butter
3 tablespoons fromage frais *or* thick cream
½ teaspoon paprika powder

Trim the chicory and split the heads in half lengthwise. Put with the split side down in a well-buttered ovenproof dish. Preheat the oven to gas mark 6, 400°F (200°C). Sprinkle the chicory with salt and pepper. Mix the cheese, breadcrumbs and parsley together in a bowl. Spread over the chicory. Trickle olive oil over the top and bake in the oven for 10 minutes. Turn down the heat to gas mark 4, 350°F (180°C). After 10 minutes, spread the fromage frais over the top and sprinkle on the paprika. Continue baking until the chicory is tender (30–40 minutes).

Courgettes

These small marrows originally came from Italy and are also known in France as *courgerons* or *coucourzelles*. They have become an important ingredient in the French cuisine, especially the southern style. They are known as *zucchini* in the United States.

Baked Courgettes
(*Courgettes au Four*)

Serves 4

4 tablespoons olive oil
1 onion, sliced
8 oz (225 g) tomatoes, chopped
8 oz (225 g) celery stalks, sliced
salt
freshly ground black pepper
2–4 cloves garlic, finely chopped
a few sage leaves
1 teaspoon chopped basil
1 lb (450 g) courgettes
3–4 tablespoons wholemeal breadcrumbs
2 tablespoons natural yogurt *or* fromage frais

Preheat the oven to gas mark 6, 400°F (200°C). In a heavy pan heat the olive oil and gently fry the onion until almost golden. Add the tomatoes and celery and turn in the oil. Season with salt and pepper to taste and add the garlic and herbs. Turn in the oil over a gentle heat until the tomatoes are tender.

Trim the courgettes and slice thinly. Arrange in a greased shallow ovenproof dish. Pour over the tomato and celery mixture and cover with the breadcrumbs. Spread with the yogurt and bake in the oven until the top is crisp and golden (25–35 minutes).

Pickled Courgettes
(*Courgettes à la Grecque*)

Serves 6

This dish uses the Greek style of marinading vegetables for use in a salad or hors d'oeuvres.

1 lb (450 g) courgettes
salt
10 fl oz (285 ml) water
5 fl oz (150 ml) olive oil
juice of 1 lemon
1 teaspoon chopped oregano
1 teaspoon chopped parsley
freshly ground black pepper
1 small onion, sliced
½ small green pepper, sliced
1 clove garlic, finely chopped
1 tomato, chopped in small pieces
12 black olives

Cut the courgettes in thick slices and boil in slightly salted water until just tender (a few minutes). Drain. In a heavy pan mix together the water, olive oil, lemon juice, herbs and salt and pepper to taste. Heat together gently for 5 minutes and allow the liquid to cool. Put the courgette slices in a bowl with the onion, green pepper and garlic and pour over the marinade. Leave to stand in a cool place for a day or overnight. Next day drain off any excess marinade and serve with tomato and olives.

Courgette Flan
(*Quiche aux Courgettes*)

Serves 4

For the pastry:
4 oz (110 g) wholewheat self-raising flour *or* 4 oz (110 g) wholewheat flour and 1 teaspoon baking powder
pinch of salt
1 oz (25 g) butter, cut in pieces
1 oz (25 g) margarine, cut in pieces
1 teaspoon soft brown sugar
3 tablespoons cold water

1 tablespoon olive oil

For the filling:
3 tablespoons olive oil
1 small onion, sliced
1 clove garlic, finely chopped
14 oz (400 g) courgettes, trimmed and sliced
salt
freshly ground black pepper
1 teaspoon chopped oregano
1 teaspoon chopped basil
2 eggs
3 tablespoons thick cream *or* natural yogurt

First make the flan pastry. Sift the flour with the salt in a mixing bowl. Add the chilled fat with a knife and stir into the flour. Make into crumbs with the fingertips. In a separate bowl dissolve the sugar in the water and stir in the oil. Gradually add this mixture to the flour until a soft, pliable dough is formed which comes away from the sides of the bowl. You may not need all of the liquid. Use flour to make into a ball. Wrap in polythene and put in the refrigerator or a cool place for 20 minutes. After 10 minutes preheat the oven to gas mark 6, 400°F (200°C).

Meanwhile make the filling. Heat the oil in a heavy pan and gently fry the onion until transparent. Add the garlic and courgettes and turn in the oil for 3 minutes. Add salt and pepper to taste and the herbs. Fry together for 5 minutes. Remove from the heat. Beat the eggs and cream together in a bowl.

Roll out the pastry on a floured board and place in a greased 8–9-inch (20–23-cm) flan tin with a removable base. Pull the pastry up the sides of the tin. Prick all over with a fork. Bake in the oven until the pastry has set (5–7 minutes). Allow to cool for a few minutes.

Arrange the courgettes in the flan base and spread the mixture over. Spoon in the egg mixture to fill in any gaps and to just cover the courgettes. Bake in the oven for 30 minutes. Allow to cool for a few minutes before removing from the tin. Serve hot or cold.

Fried Courgettes
(*Courgettes à la Meunière*)

Serves 4

The French title of this dish (in the style of the miller's wife) refers to the method of coating the vegetable slices in flour before frying.

1 lb (450 g) courgettes
wholemeal flour
oil for frying
1 tablespoon chopped parsley
lemon wedges

Trim the courgettes and cut in thick slices. Roll in the flour to coat on both sides. Fry in hot oil until golden on both sides. Drain on absorbent paper and put on a serving dish. Sprinkle over the chopped parsley and serve with lemon wedges.

Stewed Courgettes
(*Ragoût de Courgettes*)

Serves 4

4 tablespoons olive oil
1 onion, finely chopped
8 oz (225 g) tomatoes, chopped
1 lb (450 g) courgettes, trimmed and sliced
8 oz (225 g) mushrooms, sliced
2–4 cloves garlic, finely chopped
1 stick celery, sliced
handful of black olives, stoned
salt
freshly ground black pepper
2 teaspoons chopped basil
2 teaspoons chopped parsley

Heat the oil in a heavy pan and gently fry the onion until transparent. Add the tomatoes and courgettes and turn in the oil for 2 minutes. Add the mushrooms, garlic and celery and olives and cook together for a few minutes over a gentle heat. Add the salt and pepper to taste and the herbs. Cover and allow the dish to stew, adding a little water or vegetable stock if necessary.

Courgettes with Onions
(Courgettes aux Ciboules)

Serves 4

2 tablespoons olive oil
2 tablespoons melted butter
1 lb (450 g) courgettes, trimmed and sliced
salt
freshly ground black pepper
1 bunch spring onions, sliced
1 teaspoon chopped oregano
1 tablespoon chopped parsley

Heat the oil and butter in a heavy pan and lightly fry the courgettes for 2 minutes. Sprinkle on the seasoning to taste and add the onions. Turn in the oil for 3 minutes and add the herbs. Cover and cook together over a gentle heat for a few minutes until the courgettes are just tender.

Courgettes with Cream Sauce
(Courgettes à la Crème)

Serves 4

3 tablespoons melted butter
1 tablespoon olive oil
1 lb (450 g) courgettes, trimmed and sliced
salt
freshly ground black pepper
1–2 cloves garlic, finely chopped
1 cup thick cream *or* natural yogurt
½ cup vegetable stock
2 teaspoons chopped mint

Heat the butter and oil in a heavy pan and lightly fry the courgettes for 3 minutes. Sprinkle with salt and pepper to taste and add the garlic. Turn in the oil for 2 minutes. Add the cream and stock. Cover and cook over a gentle heat for a few minutes until the courgettes are just tender. Serve garnished with the chopped mint.

Courgette Gratin
(*Gratin de Courgettes*)

Serves 4

3 tablespoons olive oil
1 small onion, sliced
1 lb (450 g) courgettes, trimmed and thinly sliced
salt
freshly ground black pepper
1 tablespoon chopped parsley
2 cloves garlic, finely chopped
3 tablespoons wholemeal breadcrumbs
3 tablespoons grated gruyère *or* cheddar cheese
1 teaspoon chopped marjoram
1 egg, beaten
3 tablespoons fromage frais *or* natural yogurt
$\frac{1}{2}$ teaspoon paprika powder

Preheat the oven to gas mark 6, 400°F (200°C). Heat the oil in a heavy pan and gently fry the onion until transparent. Add the courgettes and salt and pepper to taste. Turn in the oil for 3 minutes. Add the parsley and garlic and cook together for 2 more minutes. In a separate bowl mix together the breadcrumbs, cheese, marjoram and beaten egg. Put the courgette mixture in an ovenproof dish. Spread over the breadcrumb mixture and bake in the oven for 10 minutes. Remove and spread over the fromage frais and sprinkle on the paprika. Continue baking in the oven for a further 20 minutes.

Cucumber

Cucumber Salad
(*Salade de Concombres*)

Serves 4

1 large cucumber, sliced
5 fl oz (150 ml) natural yogurt
2 tablespoons fresh chives *or* mint
salt
freshly ground black pepper

Put the cucumber in a salad bowl with the yogurt and 1 tablespoon of the herbs. Season with salt and pepper to taste. Mix together well. Garnish with the remaining herbs and serve chilled.

Cucumber with Cream Sauce
(*Concombre à la Crème*)

Serves 4

1 lb (450 g) large *or* small cucumbers
4 tablespoons melted butter
1 cup thick cream *or* natural yogurt
1 cup vegetable stock
salt
freshly ground black pepper
1 tablespoon chopped chives

Wash the cucumber and slice (lengthwise if the cucumbers are small). Heat the butter in a heavy pan and gently fry the cucumber for 2 minutes, turning the slices in the hot butter all the time. Pour in the cream, stock and sprinkle with salt and pepper to taste. Cook together on a gentle heat and do not allow to boil. When the cucumber is just tender, serve garnished with the chopped chives.

Cucumber Summer Soup
(*Potage Glacé au Concombre*)

Serves 4

1 cucumber
2 cloves garlic
1 pint (570 ml) natural yogurt
1 cup vegetable stock
1 cup dry white wine
salt
freshly ground black pepper
1 sprig tarragon
1 teaspoon finely chopped parsley

Wash the cucumber and put a few slices on one side to garnish the soup later. Chop the cucumber and purée in a blender or liquidizer with the garlic. Put in a soup pan with the yogurt, stock and wine and heat through gently. Season with salt and pepper to taste. Allow to cool after a few minutes then chill. Serve chilled and garnished with the cucumber slices and herbs.

Cucumber with Herbs
(*Concombre aux Fines Herbes*)

Serves 4

1 cucumber
salt
freshly ground black pepper
vegetable stock
1 teaspoon chopped basil
1 teaspoon chopped mint
2 tablespoons melted butter
1 tablespoon chopped parsley

Wash the cucumber and cut into short strips or dice. Put in a shallow pan and sprinkle with salt and pepper. Pour in enough stock to just cover the cucumber pieces. Sprinkle on the basil and mint and cover. Stew the dish gently for a few minutes until the cucumber is just tender. Pour off any excess moisture and put in a serving dish. Spread over the butter and serve garnished with the parsley.

Fennel

This member of the umbel family includes parsley and coriander and is of Italian origin. It is now widely cultivated, especially in the south, and the bulbous stem and leaves are used as a vegetable. It has a slight flavour of aniseed.

Fennel Provence-Style
(*Fenouil à la Provençale*)

Serves 4

This combination of garlic, herbs and a robust dry wine, such as a Côtes de Provence, produces a taste that is typically Provençale.

4 small heads fennel
salt
4 tablespoons olive oil
1 onion, finely chopped
8 oz (225 g) tomatoes, chopped
2–4 cloves garlic, finely chopped
2 teaspoons chopped basil
1 teaspoon chopped oregano
freshly ground black pepper
1 cup vegetable stock
1 cup dry wine
a few black olives, stoned

Trim the fennel and blanch in slightly salted boiling water for 15 minutes. Drain and rinse under cold water. Drain again and cut each bulb into quarters. Heat the oil in a heavy pan and gently fry the onion until it begins to turn golden. Add the tomatoes, garlic, herbs and salt and pepper to taste. Turn in the oil for 5 minutes. Put in the fennel quarters and the rest of the ingredients. Cover and cook on a gentle heat for a further 15 minutes.

Fennel Salad (*Salade de Fenouil*)   Serves 4

2 medium fennel bulbs
salt
1 tablespoon wine vinegar
freshly ground black pepper
½ teaspoon French mustard
3 tablespoons olive oil
½-1 clove garlic, finely chopped

Trim and slice the fennel bulbs. Blanch in slightly salted boiling
water for 2 minutes. Drain well. Make up the vinaigrette by
whisking together the vinegar, a pinch of salt and pepper and
the mustard. Gradually whisk in the oil and garlic until the
sauce is well blended. Toss the fennel with the vinaigrette in a
salad bowl. Cover with a cloth and allow to stand for 1 hour
before serving.

Pickled Fennel Salad   Serves 4–6
(*Fenouil à la Grecque*)

1 pint (570 ml) water
5 fl oz (150 ml) olive oil
juice of 1 lemon
1 lb (450 g) fennel
1 teaspoon fennel seeds
1 sprig parsley
1 sprig tarragon
salt
freshly ground black pepper

Mix the water, olive oil and lemon juice together in a pan. Make
sure that the pan is not affected by acids. Trim the fennel and
slice thinly. Put the green leaf in with the marinade mixture and
keep the slices on one side. Add the herbs and salt and pepper
to taste to the marinade. Heat the marinade gently for 5
minutes. Put in the fennel slices and continue heating together
for a further 5 minutes. Remove the herb sprigs and allow the
fennel to cool in the marinade overnight. Drain off most of the
marinade before serving.

Fennel Soup (*Potage au Fenouil*)　　　Serves 4–6

2 tablespoons butter
2 tablespoons olive oil
2 heads of fennel, trimmed and finely sliced
8 oz (225 g) potatoes, chopped
1 stick celery, sliced
1 clove garlic, finely chopped
2½ pints (1.43 litres) vegetable stock
1 cup natural yogurt *or* fromage frais
salt
freshly ground black pepper

Heat the butter and oil in a heavy soup pan and gently fry the
fennel for 3 minutes. Add the potatoes and celery and turn
together in the oil for a further 5 minutes. Add the garlic and
stock and simmer together for 20 minutes. Purée this mixture in
a blender or liquidizer. Return to the soup pan and stir in the
yogurt. Add seasoning to taste and gently heat through. Serve
with fried or heated bread.

　　To garnish, use a few finely chopped fennel leaves and celery
leaves.

Braised Fennel (*Fenouils Braisés*)　　　Serves 4

4 heads fennel (not too large)
4 tablespoons butter
salt
freshly ground black pepper
1 teaspoon chopped chives
1 teaspoon chopped parsley
1 teaspoon chopped tarragon

Trim the fennel and save a little of the fresh leaves as a garnish.
Blanch in slightly salted boiling water for 15 minutes. Remove
and rinse under cold water and allow to drain. Cut each bulb
into quarters. Heat the butter in a heavy pan and gently braise
the fennel quarters until they just begin to turn golden. Sprinkle
with salt and pepper to taste and serve garnished with the
chopped herbs, including the fresh fennel leaf.

French Beans

French Bean Salad
(*Salade d'Haricots Verts*)

Serves 4

1 lb (450 g) young French beans
salt
olive oil
wine vinegar
freshly ground black pepper
2 teaspoons chopped tarragon
1 teaspoon chopped chives

Trim the beans and boil in slightly salted water until just tender (a few minutes only). Drain. Make up a vinaigrette dressing to taste with olive oil, vinegar, salt and pepper. Pour over just enough to cover the beans and turn them in the dressing. Arrange on a serving dish and garnish with the chopped herbs. The beans can be eaten warm or allowed to chill for 30 minutes.

French Beans with Garlic
(*Haricots Verts à l'Ail*)

Serves 4

1 lb (450 g) French Beans
salt
4 tablespoons melted butter
2–4 cloves garlic, finely chopped
2 tablespoons wholemeal breadcrumbs
freshly ground black pepper
a few finely chopped sage leaves

Trim the beans. Make sure they are firm and snap when broken. Break the beans in half. Blanch in slightly salted boiling water until just tender (about 10 minutes). Drain. Heat the butter in a heavy pan and gently fry the garlic for 2 minutes. Add the breadcrumbs and season with salt and pepper to taste. Fry together until the breadcrumbs begin to crisp. Do not allow the butter to burn. Remove from the heat and put in the beans. Turn quickly in the garlic butter. Serve garnished with the chopped herb.

French Beans with Turnips
(*Haricots Verts aux Navets*)

Serves 4

8 oz (225 g) turnip
10 oz (285 g) French beans
salt
2 tablespoons melted butter
2 tablespoons olive oil
1 onion, sliced
8 oz (225 g) tomatoes, chopped
freshly ground black pepper
$\frac{1}{2}$ cup dry wine

Peel the turnip and cut into small pieces. Trim the beans and snap in half. Cook both vegetables in separate pans of slightly salted water until they are almost tender. Remove the vegetables and keep the liquid on one side. Heat the butter and oil in a heavy pan and gently fry the onion until transparent. Add the tomatoes and turn in the oil for 5 minutes. Add the par-cooked vegetables and season with salt and pepper to taste. Add the wine and any of the liquid necessary from the par-cooked vegetables to make a sauce. Cover and cook over a gentle heat for 10 minutes.

French Beans with Mushrooms
(*Haricots Verts au Forestier*)

Serves 4

The title of the dish refers to the wild mushrooms that grow in woods and forests and which form a natural part of the country cuisine in such areas. Use any large mushrooms that may be available.

1 lb (450 g) French beans
salt
3 tablespoons melted butter
1 tablespoon olive oil
8 oz (225 g) mushrooms, sliced
2–4 cloves garlic, sliced
freshly ground black pepper
2 teaspoons chopped parsley

Trim the beans and snap in half. Blanch in slightly salted boiling water until just tender. Drain. Heat the butter and oil in a heavy pan and gently fry the mushrooms for 2 minutes. Add the garlic and season with salt and pepper to taste. Fry together for 3 minutes. Add the beans and turn in the mushrooms for a further 3 minutes. Serve garnished with chopped parsley or any herb to hand.

French Beans with Tomatoes
(*Haricots Verts aux Tomates*)

Serves 4

2 tablespoons melted butter
2 tablespoons olive oil
2–4 cloves garlic, sliced
1 lb (450 g) French beans, trimmed and sliced
10 oz (285 g) tomatoes, chopped
1 tablespoon chopped basil
1 tablespoon chopped parsley
salt
freshly ground black pepper
1 cup vegetable stock
1 cup dry red wine

Heat the butter and oil in a heavy pan and gently fry the garlic for 2 minutes. Add the beans, tomatoes, herbs and salt and pepper to taste. Turn in the oil for 5 minutes. Add the stock and wine and cover. Cook over a gentle heat for 10–15 minutes.

French Bean Gratin
(*Gratin de Haricots Verts*)

Serves 4

1 lb (450 g) French beans
salt
2 tablespoons melted butter
8 oz (225 g) small mushrooms, sliced thickly
freshly ground black pepper
2 teaspoons chopped parsley
3 tablespoons wholemeal breadcrumbs
2 tablespoons grated gruyère *or* cheddar cheese
1 teaspoon chopped rosemary leaf
2 tablespoons olive oil

Trim the beans and snap in half. Blanch in slightly salted boiling water for 5 minutes. Drain. Preheat the oven to gas mark 6, 400°F (200°C). Heat the butter in a heavy pan and gently fry the mushrooms for 2 minutes. Season with salt and pepper to taste and stir in the parsley. Add the beans and turn in the butter for 3 minutes. Put in a greased ovenproof dish. Mix together the breadcrumbs, cheese and rosemary leaf and spread over the bean and mushroom mixture. Trickle over the oil and bake in the oven for 30 minutes or until the top is crisp and golden.

Garlic

This excellent vegetable is the base of most of the southern-style cuisine, particularly the Provençale style. Well known for its health-promoting properties, it used to be carried by doctors in the sixteenth and seventeenth centuries as a guard against contracting infections.

Garlic Soup (*Soup à l'Ail*)   Serves 4

4 tablespoons olive oil
1 large onion *or* 2 small leeks, sliced
8 oz (225 g) tomatoes, chopped
2 potatoes, chopped
4 cloves garlic, crushed
2½ pints (1.43 litres) vegetable stock
½ cup wine
salt
freshly ground black pepper
1 teaspoon chopped basil
1 teaspoon chopped parsley

Heat the oil in a heavy soup pan and gently fry the onion until just golden. Add the tomatoes, potatoes and garlic and turn in the oil for 5 minutes. Add the stock and the rest of the ingredients. Cover and cook for 20 minutes. Check the seasoning. Add more crushed garlic if necessary.

Serve with fried or warmed crusty bread. This can be done southern-style by putting the bread in the soup bowl and pouring the soup over it.

Garlic and Walnut Dip (*Aïllade Toulousaine*)

This relative of Aïoli comes from the walnut-growing regions of the Languedoc and Dordogne. Ideally fresh walnuts should be used, but the addition of walnut oil helps to make the authentic taste and aroma with any good walnuts. Use in the same way as Aïoli with raw or cooked vegetables and crusty bread.

4 cloves garlic
pinch of salt
3–4 tablespoons shelled walnuts
$\frac{1}{2}$ cup walnut oil *or* olive oil

Pound the garlic and salt then add the walnuts and pound together until a smooth paste is formed. Gradually add the oil, pounding continuously to make a thick sauce. Use the same day.

Garlic Mayonnaise (*Aïoli*)

In Provence, the last big meal before Lent used to be Aïoli. This is used as a garnish for a variety of cooked ingredients such as fennel, onions, carrots, French beans, artichokes, unskinned potatoes, hard-boiled eggs and herbs. Arrange them tastefully on a dish and serve with the garlic mayonnaise.

4–6 cloves garlic
1 egg yolk
pinch of salt
1 cup olive oil
freshly ground black pepper (optional)

Pound the garlic and egg yolk together to make a paste. Season with salt. Gradually add the oil, drop by drop, pounding it into the paste. Season with pepper. Continue pounding until a smooth thick mayonnaise is made.

Haricot Beans

Soak and cook dried haricot beans in the same way as described for chick peas.

Haricot Bean Salad (*Salade de Haricots*)   Serves 4

3 cups cooked haricot beans
1 small onion, finely sliced
2 sticks celery, sliced
salt
freshly ground black pepper
4 tablespoons olive oil
juice of 1 lemon
1 tablespoon chopped parsley
2 tomatoes, cut in small pieces

Put the beans in a salad bowl and mix with the rest of the ingredients. Serve at room temperature or slightly chilled. Other herbs such as tarragon or sage could be substituted for the parsley.

Haricot Bean Soup (*Potage de Haricots*)   Serves 4

At the time of Pentecost (Pentecôte), a haricot bean soup called 'the soup of the Holy Ghost' is the traditional dish in the village of La Croix in the Alpes-Maritimes. It is made in two 33-gallon (150-litre) cauldrons in the local church.

3 tablespoons olive oil
1 onion, finely chopped
2 carrots, peeled and sliced
2 tomatoes, chopped

2 cups cooked haricot beans
2 bay leaves
1 teaspoon chopped basil
1 teaspoon chopped sage
salt
freshly ground black pepper
2½ pints (1.43 litres) vegetable stock *or* water
½ cup thick cream *or* yogurt

Heat the oil in a heavy soup pan and fry the onion until just golden. Add the carrots and tomatoes and turn in the hot oil for 5 minutes. Add the cooked beans, herbs and salt and pepper to taste. Stir together and add the stock. Cover and cook together over a gentle heat for 15 minutes. Purée the soup in a blender or liquidizer and return to the pan. Stir in the cream and heat gently. Do not allow the soup to boil. Serve with fried or warmed bread.

Haricot Bean Gratin
(*Gratin de Haricots Blancs*)

Serves 4

2 tablespoons olive oil
2 tablespoons melted butter
1 onion, finely chopped
2 cups cooked haricot beans
salt
freshly ground black pepper
6 oz (170 g) mushrooms, sliced
6–8 black olives, stoned (optional)
1 teaspoon chopped sage
1 teaspoon chopped parsley
3 tablespoons wholemeal breadcrumbs
2 tablespoons fromage frais *or* natural yogurt

Preheat the oven to gas mark 6, 400°F (200°C). Heat the oil and butter in a heavy pan and fry the onion until transparent. Add the beans and turn in the oil for 3 minutes. Season with salt and pepper to taste and add the mushrooms, olives and herbs. Cook together for 5 minutes. Put into a greased ovenproof dish and spread with the breadcrumbs. Spread over the fromage frais and bake in the oven until the top is firm (15–20 minutes).

Haricot Beans Poitou-Style
(*Haricots à la Poitevinne*)

The gastronomic area of Poitou is rich in agricultural produce and includes the départements of Vendée, Vienne, Deux-Sèvres and Maine-et-Loire.

1 onion, stuck with 2 cloves
1 large carrot, peeled and sliced
2 sticks celery, sliced
1 small parsnip *or* piece of swede, sliced
2 cloves garlic, sliced
salt
freshly ground black pepper
1 teaspoon chopped thyme
1 teaspoon chopped marjoram
3 cups cooked haricot beans
½ cup cream *or* natural yogurt
2 teaspoons chopped parsley
2 teaspoons chopped basil

Put the onion, carrot, celery, parsnip and garlic in a pan and sprinkle with salt and pepper to taste. Cover with water and stir in the thyme and marjoram. Cover and allow to cook together over a gentle heat until all the vegetables are tender. Drain. The cooking liquid may be used as stock. Put all the vegetables back in the pan. Remove the cloves from the onion and slice. Add the beans and cream. Turn together over a gentle heat, adding a little of the cooking liquid if necessary to make a sauce. Serve garnished with the chopped parsley and basil.

Southern Bean Stew
(*Cassoulet aux Légumes*)

The term *cassoulet* comes from *cassoule*, a glazed earthenware casserole, reddish in colour, made near Castelnaudary in the ancient region of Languedoc. This cassoulet is an adaption of the traditional dish. You can vary the ingredients to suit your taste, but typically it should include haricot beans.

2 tablespoons olive oil
1 tablespoon melted butter
1 onion, chopped
8 oz (225 g) carrots, chopped
2–4 cloves garlic, finely chopped
handful of mixed herbs
6 oz (170 g) cooked haricot beans
6 oz (170 g) cooked chick peas
6 oz (170 g) French beans, snapped in pieces
2–4 tomatoes, chopped
4 oz (110 g) frozen *or* par-cooked fresh peas
8 oz (225 g) courgettes, chopped
½ pint (285 ml) vegetable stock
salt
freshly ground black pepper
4 oz (110 g) wholemeal breadcrumbs

Preheat the oven to gas mark 6, 400°F (200°C). Heat the oil and butter in a casserole dish and gently fry the onion until transparent. Add the carrots, garlic, herbs, beans and chick peas and cook together for 5 minutes. Add the tomatoes, peas, courgettes and stock. Season with salt and pepper to taste and cook together for 20 minutes. Cover with the breadcrumbs and bake in the oven until the top is crisp and golden (about 15 minutes).

Haricot Beans with Basil and Garlic (*Haricots au Pistou*)

Serves 4

4 tablespoons olive oil
1 onion, sliced
8 oz (225 g) tomatoes, chopped
2–4 cloves garlic, sliced
3 cups par-cooked haricot beans
salt
freshly ground black pepper
1 teaspoon chopped thyme
1 teaspoon chopped marjoram
vegetable stock

For the pistou:
4 cloves garlic
handful of fresh basil leaves
$\frac{1}{2}$ cup olive oil

Heat the oil in a heavy pan and gently fry the onion until transparent. Add the tomatoes and garlic and turn in the oil for 5 minutes. Add the beans, salt and pepper to taste, thyme, marjoram and enough stock to cover the vegetables. Cover and cook on a gentle heat until the beans are tender.

Meanwhile make the pistou. Pound the garlic with the basil leaves to make a paste. Gradually add the olive oil, pounding to make a thick sauce. When the beans are cooked, stir into the pan and mix together well.

Herbs

Since medieval times herbs have found a special place in European cooking. It has always been the custom both to collect wild herbs for culinary use as well as to grow them in the garden as potherbs. Cultivated herbs for kitchen use are known as *fines herbes*. The collection of herbs known as *bouquet garni* consists of thyme, parsley, marjoram and basil wrapped in a cloth packet. People vary both the ingredients and the quantities to make up the bouquet garni. Many cooks remove the herb packet after it has served its purpose of aromatizing the ingredients of the dish. Herbs present a lovely range of plants with which to experiment for taste, aroma and colour. Use the following recipes as a basis for your own variations.

Herb Salad (*Salade Verte*)   Serves 4

1 lb (450 g) lettuce and other salad greens such as dandelion
    leaves, chicory, watercress, borage, sorrel or rocket
1 tablespoon wine vinegar *or* 2 teaspoons lemon juice
pinch of salt
freshly ground black pepper
½ teaspoon French mustard
3 tablespoons olive oil
½–1 clove garlic, crushed
2 tablespoons chopped fresh herbs such as basil, parsley,
    chives, chervil, tarragon, marjoram or chopped fennel leaf

Wash the salad greens and tear in pieces. Dry thoroughly. Make the vinaigrette by whisking the vinegar with the salt, pepper and mustard. Gradually add the oil and garlic and whisk together until the sauce is well blended. Toss with the greens just before they are required. Sprinkle with the chopped herbs. The vinaigrette may be adjusted to suit individual tastes.

Herb Soup (*Potage aux Fines Herbes*) Serves 4

4 oz (110 g) potatoes, chopped
2½ pints (1.43 litres) vegetable stock
salt
freshly ground black pepper
3–4 tablespoons melted butter
4 oz (110 g) lettuce, chopped
4 oz (110 g) sorrel, chopped
4 oz (110 g) dandelion leaves, chopped
2 tablespoons chopped chives
1 tablespoon chopped parsley

Put the potatoes in a large soup pan with the stock. Season with salt and pepper to taste and bring to the boil. Cover and simmer over a gentle heat until the potatoes are soft. Mash the potatoes to thicken the stock. In a separate pan heat the butter and add the lettuce, sorrel, dandelion, chives and parsley. Turn in the butter over a gentle heat for 3 minutes. Pour the whole into the soup pan and heat together. Check the seasoning and serve hot with fried or warmed bread.

Basil

Basil was once considered a royal plant and only the sovereign (*basileus*) was allowed to cut it. This was done with a golden sickle. The aromatic leaves are an essential ingredient in the Provençal flavouring *pistou*.

Basil and Garlic Soup (*Soupe au Pistou*) Serves 6

Pistou is the French relative of the Genovese *pesto* which also includes pounded pine nuts. Since the pounded pommade may be added to the soup just before consumption, it can add fun to a meal where each guest can help themselves from the communal bowl. This recipe is ideal for using up any vegetables that are to hand as well as any broken pasta that you are wondering what to do with.

3 tablespoons olive oil
1 onion, sliced
6 oz (170 g) carrots, cut in small pieces
12 oz (350 g) potatoes, cut in small chunks
10 oz (285 g) pumpkin, cut in chunks
2 leeks, trimmed and sliced
1 lb (450 g) haricot beans
8 oz (225 g) broad beans
2 teaspoons chopped thyme
2 teaspoons chopped marjoram
1 tablespoon chopped parsley
salt
freshly ground black pepper
3½ pints (2 litres) water
8 oz (225 g) French beans, sliced
8 oz (225 g) courgettes, sliced
4 oz (110 g) broken pasta *or* macaroni

For the pistou:
4 cloves garlic
good handful fresh basil
2–4 oz (60–110 g) grated parmesan cheese
1 cup olive oil

Heat the oil in a large soup pan and gently fry the onion until transparent. Add the carrots, potatoes, pumpkin, leeks, beans, herbs, salt and pepper to taste. Heat the water while you stir the vegetables in the oil. Pour in the water. Cover and simmer until the vegetables are just tender. Add the green beans, courgettes and pasta and cook together for 10 minutes.

While the soup is cooking make the pistou. Pound the garlic in a mortar with the basil until the herb is well pulped. Add a little cheese and pound together. Keep adding the cheese until all the cheese is used up. Now gradually add the oil the same way until a thick cream is formed. Add to the soup just before serving or put in the middle of the table for people to serve themselves. Serve the soup with chunky bread and perhaps a bowl of olives. This dish makes a meal by itself.

Basil and Tomato with Scrambled Eggs   Serves 4
(*Tomates au Basilic avec Oeufs Brouillés*)

4 tablespoons olive oil
4 tomatoes, chopped
2–3 cloves garlic, finely chopped
1 tablespoon chopped basil
1 tablespoon melted butter
8 eggs
salt
freshly ground black pepper
1 tablespoon chopped chives

Heat the oil in a heavy pan and gently fry the tomatoes for 5 minutes. Add the garlic and basil and continue frying until the tomatoes are nicely softened. Add the butter to the eggs in a bowl and beat together. Pour into the tomato mixture and stir in with a fork. Sprinkle with salt and pepper to taste and continue stirring with the fork until the desired consistency is obtained. Serve each portion garnished with a little chopped chives.

Chervil

Chervil has been cultivated as a potherb in France for many centuries. It should have stiff stems and a curly leaf. Do not use limp chervil.

Chervil and Scrambled Eggs   Serves 4
(*Cerfeuil aux Oeufs Brouillés*)

8 eggs
salt
freshly ground black pepper
2 tablespoons chopped chervil
3 oz (85 g) butter

Whisk the eggs with salt and pepper to taste until slightly frothy. Beat in the chervil. Melt the butter in a heavy pan over a gentle heat. Add the eggs and stir constantly with a wooden spoon until they begin to thicken. Cook as slowly as possible. Remove from the heat while the eggs are still moist. Serve on slices of toast or bread fried in oil.

Dandelion

Known in France as *pissenlit* because of its diuretic properties, dandelion has been a popular wild herb for many centuries. Larger dandelion leaf is often cultivated in gardens for use as a potherb. Gather the leaves when young and not too dark green and bitter.

Dandelion and Egg Salad   Serves 4
(*Salade de Pissenlit aux Oeufs*)

1 lb (450 g) dandelion leaves
1 clove garlic, finely chopped
2–4 eggs, hard-boiled
salt
freshly ground black pepper
olive oil
wine vinegar
2 tomatoes, sliced

Wash the dandelion leaves and dry well. Tear into pieces with the fingers and mix together with the garlic. Arrange in a salad bowl with the eggs which can be sliced or cut in halves. Sprinkle with salt and pepper to taste. Serve with olive oil and vinegar to taste and garnish with tomato slices.

Dandelion with Cheese and Walnuts
(*Salade de Pissenlit au Roquefort*)

Serves 4

10 oz (285 g) dandelion leaves
4 oz (110 g) roquefort *or* other blue cheese
1 clove garlic, finely chopped
a few spring onions, sliced finely
salt
freshly ground black pepper
2 tablespoons chopped walnuts
a few sage leaves
olive oil *or* walnut oil
wine vinegar *or* lemon juice

Wash the dandelion leaves and dry well. Arrange in a salad bowl and add the cheese, garlic, spring onions and sprinkle with salt and pepper to taste. Add the nuts and sage leaves and allow to stand for 30 minutes. Serve with an oil and vinegar dressing to taste.

Sorrel

This hardy perenniel herb was known in Asia before 300 BC. It was known in France during the thirteenth century as one of the English herbs and still grows wild.

Sorrel Soup (*Soupe à l'Oseille*)

Serves 4

8 oz (225 g) young sorrel leaves
3 tablespoons melted butter
1 onion, sliced
1 lb (450 g) potatoes, chopped
salt
freshly ground black pepper
2½ pints (1.43 litres) vegetable stock
2 tablespoons chopped chives

Wash the sorrel leaves and remove any coarse stalks. Slice. Heat the butter in a heavy soup pan and gently fry the onion until transparent. Add the potatoes and turn in the hot butter for 3 minutes. Add the sorrel and turn again for 2 minutes. Season with salt and pepper to taste and add the stock. Cover and cook over a gentle heat until the potatoes are tender. Mash them to thicken the soup. Serve garnished with chopped chives and crusty bread.

Braised Sorrel (*Oseille Braisée*)   Serves 4

$1\frac{1}{2}$ lb (675 g) young sorrel leaves
3 tablespoons melted butter
salt
freshly ground black pepper
freshly grated nutmeg

Wash the sorrel leaves and remove any coarse stalks. Slice. Heat the butter in a heavy pan and gently fry the sorrel until the leaves soften. Season with salt, pepper and nutmeg to taste. Serve with fried or warm crusty bread.

Sorrel Omelette (*Omelette à l'Oseille*)   Serves 2

4 oz (110 g) young sorrel leaves
butter
salt
freshly ground black pepper
4 eggs, beaten
2 tablespoons fromage frais *or* natural yogurt
freshly grated nutmeg

Wash the sorrel and remove any coarse stalks. Slice. Heat 2 tablespoons of butter in a heavy pan and gently fry the sorrel for 2 minutes. Season with salt and pepper. Remove from the heat. Coat the bottom of an omelette pan with melted butter and pour in the eggs. When they begin to solidify, stir the fromage frais into the sorrel. Put in the middle of the omelette. Sprinkle on some grated nutmeg. Allow the omelette to thicken. Remove from the pan just before the egg is completely solid.

Sorrel with Cream Sauce
(*Oseille à la Crème*)

Serves 4

1½ lb (675 g) young sorrel leaves
salt
3 tablespoons melted butter
freshly grated nutmeg
½ cup thick cream *or* fromage frais
fried cooked potatoes
1 tablespoon chopped parsley

Wash the sorrel and remove any coarse stalks. Blanch in boiling slightly salted water for 5 minutes. Slice. Heat the butter in a heavy pan and add the drained sorrel. Turn in the hot butter for 2 minutes. Season with nutmeg and stir in the cream. Put in the middle of a serving dish. Surround with fried potatoes which are garnished with parsley.

Watercress

Watercress is such a strong-tasting herb that it is best prepared on its own without the addition of other herbs. Below is a simple country recipe that can be prepared in a few minutes.

Watercress with Cream
(*Cresson à la Crème*)

Serves 4

12 oz (350 g) watercress
3 tablespoons melted butter
salt
freshly ground black pepper
1 tablespoon dry wine
1 tablespoon vegetable stock
2 tablespoons fromage frais *or* natural yoghurt
2 tablespoons cream

Wash the watercress and drain well. Heat the butter in a heavy pan and put in the watercress. Season with salt and pepper and turn in the hot butter for 3 minutes. Add the wine and stock, then the fromage frais and cream. Cook together over a low heat but do not allow the mixture to bubble. Serve after 2 minutes.

Watercress Soup (*Potage au Cresson*)   Serves 4

1 large bunch watercress
3 tablespoons melted butter
salt
freshly ground black pepper
freshly grated nutmeg
2 eggs
2 tablespoons grated parmesan cheese
2½ pints (1.43 litres) vegetable stock
2 tablespoons grated gruyère *or* cheddar cheese

Wash the watercress well and chop. Heat the butter in a heavy soup pan and add the watercress. Turn in the hot butter for 3 minutes. Season with salt, pepper and nutmeg to taste. In a separate bowl, beat the eggs and beat in the cheese. Put the stock in the soup pan and bring to the boil. Add a cup of stock to the egg and cheese mixture. Stir together and add to the soup. Do not allow the soup to boil. Serve garnished with the cheese.

Leeks

Leek and Potato Soup
(*Potage Fermière*)

Serves 4–6

This soup is typical of the simple, substantial dishes which were prepared in the homes of farmers and smallholders. Such dishes form the basis of good country cookery.

8 oz (225 g) leeks
8 oz (225 g) potatoes
8 oz (225 g) carrots *or* parsnips
3 tablespoons butter
1 onion, finely chopped
2½ pints (1.43 litres) water *or* vegetable stock
salt
freshly ground black pepper
½ cup thick cream *or* yogurt
1 tablespoon finely chopped parsley

Trim the leeks and wash well. Clean the potatoes and trim the carrots. Chop all the vegetables. Heat the butter in a heavy soup pan and gently fry the onion until transparent. Add the chopped vegetables and turn in the butter for 3 minutes. Add the stock and season with salt and pepper to taste. Cover and simmer for 20 minutes. Remove from the heat and stir in the cream. Return to the heat but do not allow the dish to boil. If you have a cup of dry wine available this may be added to the soup also. Serve garnished with chopped parsley.

This soup may be puréed by passing through a blender or liquidizer before the cream is added.

Leek and Vegetable Soup
(*Potage aux Poireaux et Légumes*)

Serves 6

3 tablespoons olive oil
1 tablespoon melted butter
1 onion, finely chopped
2 good-sized leeks
4 oz (110 g) French beans, sliced
2 carrots, sliced
2 sticks celery, sliced
4 oz (110 g) tomatoes, chopped
salt
freshly ground black pepper
2 bay leaves
1 teaspoon chopped oregano
1 teaspoon chopped marjoram
$2\frac{1}{2}$ pints (1.43 litres) vegetable stock *or* water
$\frac{1}{2}$–1 cup dry wine
$\frac{1}{2}$ cup thick cream
1 tablespoon finely chopped parsley *or* chervil

Heat the oil and butter in a heavy soup pan and gently fry the onion until transparent. Add the leeks which have been trimmed, well washed and chopped and stir in the oil. Add the beans, carrots, celery and tomatoes. Season with salt and pepper to taste, bay leaf, oregano and marjoram. Turn in the oil for 3 minutes. Add the stock and wine. Cover and cook together until all the vegetables are well cooked. Serve hot with a little cream and chopped parsley on the top.

Leek Purée (*Purée de Poireaux*)

Serves 6

$2\frac{1}{2}$ lb (1.12 kg) leeks
salt
4 tablespoons melted butter
freshly ground black pepper
$\frac{1}{2}$ cup thick cream *or* natural yogurt
1 teaspoon chopped tarragon

Trim the leeks and wash well. Chop and put in a pan with just enough water to cover. Sprinkle with a little salt and boil until the leeks are just tender. Drain. The liquid may be used for stock or soup-making. Heat the butter in a heavy pan and turn the leeks in the hot butter for 2 minutes. Put in a blender or liquidizer and purée. Put in a serving dish and stir in the cream. Serve garnished with the chopped tarragon.

Leeks and Mushrooms with Cream Sauce
(*Poireaux à la Crème*)   Serves 4

1 lb (450 g) leeks
salt
2 tablespoons olive oil
2 tablespoons melted butter
8 oz (225 g) mushrooms, finely chopped
freshly ground black pepper
1–2 cloves garlic, finely chopped
$\frac{1}{2}$ cup dry white wine
$\frac{1}{2}$ cup natural yogurt *or* fromage frais
5 fl oz (150 ml) thick cream
pinch of freshly grated nutmeg
1 teaspoon chopped chives *or* parsley

Trim the leeks and wash well. Chop and boil in slightly salted water until just tender. Drain and retain the leek liquid. Heat the oil and butter in a heavy pan and gently fry the chopped mushrooms for 2 minutes. Sprinkle with salt and pepper to taste and add the garlic. Fry together for 3 minutes. Add the wine and yogurt and heat together until well blended. Add the cream and stir together. Add any of the leek liquid if necessary to make a thin sauce. Put in the leeks and heat through but do not allow the sauce to boil. Put in a serving dish and sprinkle with grated nutmeg and chopped herbs.

Leeks Savoy-Style
(*Poireaux à la Savoyarde*)

Serves 4

Lying between the Rhône Valley and the Alpine borders of Switzerland and Italy, is the old province of Savoie. Here, leeks are treated to a delicate aromatization with pepper, nutmeg, spring onions and parsley.

1 lb (450 g) leeks
2 sticks celery
salt
2 oz (60 g) butter
4–6 spring onions, sliced
freshly ground black pepper
1 tablespoon chopped parsley
4 tablespoons wholemeal breadcrumbs
4 tablespoons grated gruyère *or* cheddar cheese
freshly grated nutmeg
2 tablespoons olive oil

Trim the leeks and celery and wash well. Chop and boil the vegetables together in slightly salted water until the leeks are just tender. Preheat the oven to gas mark 6, 400°F (200°C). Heat the butter in a separate pan and gently fry the spring onions for 3 minutes. Season with salt and pepper to taste. Add the drained leeks, parsley and half of the breadcrumbs. Fry together for 5 minutes. Put in a greased ovenproof dish. Mix together the rest of the breadcrumbs, cheese and nutmeg. Spread over the top of the leek mixture. Sprinkle with olive oil and bake in the oven until the top is crisp and golden (15–20 minutes).

Lentils

Lentils with Mustard Sauce
(*Lentilles à la Dijonnaise*)

Serves 4

This dish takes its name from the particular type of Dijon mustard which is used. This is the spicy mustard with whole mustard grains.

1½ cups lentils
2 tablespoons olive oil
2 tablespoons melted butter
1 onion, sliced
1–2 cloves garlic, crushed
8 oz (225 g) tomatoes, chopped
1 tablespoon chopped parsley
salt
freshly ground black pepper
3 cups vegetable stock
1 cup dry red wine
1–2 tablespoons Dijon mustard
2 tablespoons fromage frais *or* natural yogurt

Wash the lentils in plenty of cold water and drain. Heat the oil and butter in a heavy pan and gently fry the onion until transparent. Add the garlic, tomatoes, parsley and salt and pepper to taste. Stir together for 5 minutes. Gradually add the stock, wine and lentils and cook on a low heat until tender, adding more stock if necessary. Stir in half of the mustard and taste. If a good mustard taste is preferred, add the rest. Stir in the fromage frais and heat through. Do not allow the dish to boil.

Lentil Purée
(*Purée de Lentilles*)

Serves 4–6

2 cups lentils
1 carrot, peeled and chopped
2 potatoes, chopped
1 onion, chopped
salt
freshly ground black pepper
2 bay leaves
1 teaspoon chopped marjoram
1 teaspoon chopped thyme
2 teaspoons chopped parsley
lemon wedges

Wash the lentils and leave to soak in water while you prepare
the vegetables. It is not necessary to soak lentils overnight.
Drain the lentils and put in a pan with the prepared vegetables.
Sprinkle with salt and pepper to taste and add the herbs. Cover
with cold water and bring to the boil. Simmer together over a
gentle heat until all the vegetables are tender. Purée in a blender
or liquidizer. Serve with lemon wedges and crusty bread.

Lentils with Spinach
(*Lentilles aux Épinards*)

Serves 4

2 cups lentils
2 tablespoons olive oil
2 tablespoons melted butter
1 onion, finely chopped
8 oz (225 g) tomatoes, chopped
salt
freshly ground black pepper
1 bay leaf
1 teaspoon chopped parsley
1 lb (450 g) spinach
1–2 cloves garlic, finely chopped

Wash the lentils and leave to soak in cold water. Heat the oil and butter in a heavy pan and gently fry the onion until it begins to turn golden. Add the tomatoes and turn in the oil for 3 minutes. Season with salt and pepper to taste and add the bay leaf and parsley. Stir together for a further 3 minutes. Drain the lentils and put in the pan with the tomato mixture. Cover with warm water and allow to cook until the lentils are almost tender, adding more water as necessary.

Wash the spinach and tear the leaf away from the thick stalks. Put in with the lentils. Add the garlic and allow to cook together until the spinach is tender (a few minutes).

Lettuce

Lettuce and Cheese Salad
(Salade aux Fromages de Chèvre)   Serves 4

1 crisp lettuce
good handful of young dandelion leaves
olive oil
wine vinegar *or* lemon juice
salt
freshly ground black pepper
1 teaspoon French mustard
handful of chopped fresh herbs
8 oz (225 g) goat's milk cheese, sliced

Wash the lettuce and dry well. Arrange in a bowl with the dandelion leaves. Make up a vinaigrette sauce by whisking together the oil, vinegar, salt, pepper and mustard to taste. Just before the salad is required, toss the lettuce and dandelion with the vinaigrette. Sprinkle with the herbs and arrange slices of goat's cheese on the salad.

Braised Lettuce (*Laitues Braisées*)   Serves 4

4 small crisp lettuces
salt
2 tablespoons melted butter
1 medium onion, finely chopped
1 cup hot vegetable stock
1 teaspoon chopped marjoram
1 teaspoon chopped thyme
freshly ground black pepper
wholemeal flour

Preheat the oven to gas mark 5, 375°F (190°C). Wash the lettuces and trim off any damaged outer leaves.

Put the lettuces head down in a pan of boiling slightly salted water and blanch for 5 minutes. Remove and drain and cut each lettuce in halves or quarters. Heat the butter in a casserole and gently fry the onion until it begins to turn golden. Put the drained lettuce pieces on top of the onion. Pour over the stock and sprinkle with the herbs and salt and pepper to taste. Cover and put in the oven for 30 minutes. Remove the lettuces, put on a serving dish and keep warm. Thicken the sauce over a gentle heat by stirring in a teaspoon or two of flour. Pour over the lettuces.

Lettuce with Mushrooms   Serves 4
(*Laitues aux Champignons*)

4 small crisp lettuces
salt
2 tablespoons olive oil
1 tablespoon melted butter
1 onion, finely chopped
8 oz (225 g) small mushrooms, sliced
freshly ground black pepper
1–2 cloves garlic, finely chopped
$\frac{1}{2}$ cup dry wine
1 teaspoon chopped basil
1 teaspoon chopped parsley
2 tablespoons cream *or* fromage frais

Trim the lettuces and discard any damaged outer leaves. Wash well and put head down in a pan of boiling slightly salted water. Blanch for 5 minutes and drain well. Cut into halves or quarters. Keep warm. Heat the oil and butter in a heavy pan and gently fry the onion until transparent. Add the mushrooms and turn in the oil for 3 minutes. Add a little salt and pepper to season and the garlic. Fry together for a further 3 minutes. Add the wine, herbs and cream and heat through. Do not allow the sauce to boil. Put the lettuces on a serving dish and pour over the mushroom sauce.

Buckwheat Pancakes with Lettuce and Cheese Sauce
(*Galettes de Sarrasin à la Laitue*) Serves 4–8

Buckwheat is thought to have been introduced into France by the Crusaders, hence its name 'Saracen'. Its ground seeds make a dark, nourishing flour. In Brittany these crêpes are known as *galettes*.

For the crêpes:
1 egg
8 fl oz (225 ml) milk
½ teaspoon salt
5 oz (150 g) buckwheat flour
butter for frying

For the filling:
1 large crisp lettuce
2 eggs, beaten
4 oz (110 g) natural yogurt
2 oz (60 g) roquefort *or* cheddar cheese, crumbled *or* grated
2 tablespoons cream *or* fromage frais
1 teaspoon Dijon mustard
freshly ground black pepper
chopped chives *or* parsley to garnish

Make the batter by beating together the egg, milk and salt. Gradually add the buckwheat flour and beat in until smooth. Leave to stand.

Wash the lettuce and chop. Make the sauce by mixing together the eggs, yogurt, cheese, cream and mustard in a heavy pan. Heat over a pan of boiling water until the sauce thickens. Season with pepper to taste and keep warm.

Make the pancakes by heating a little butter in a heavy pan. Pour off the excess. Add a spoonful of batter to cover the bottom of the pan. Allow the pancake to brown on both sides. Turn out onto a plate.

Fill each pancake with chopped lettuce and a little sauce. Roll up and arrange on a serving dish. Pour over the rest of the sauce and garnish with chopped herbs.

Marrow

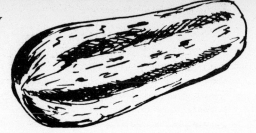

Marrow Provence-Style
(*Courge à la Provençale*)

Serves 4

1 2–3 lb (900g–1.35 kg) marrow
3 tablespoons olive oil
1 tablespoon melted butter
1 onion, sliced
1 lb (450 g) tomatoes, chopped
2–4 cloves garlic, finely chopped
1 teaspoon chopped basil
1 teaspoon chopped oregano
2 teaspoons chopped parsley
salt
freshly ground black pepper
1 cup vegetable stock
1 cup dry red wine

Peel the marrow, remove the seeds and cut into small chunks or slices. Heat the oil and butter in a heavy pan and gently fry the onion until transparent. Add the tomatoes and garlic and turn in the oil for 3 minutes. Add the marrow pieces, herbs and salt and pepper to taste. Turn in the oil for 5 minutes. Add the stock and wine and cook together until the marrow is tender. Carry on cooking if you want the sauce to thicken.

Baked Marrow (*Courge au Four*)   Serves 4

1 2–3 lb (900 g–1.35 kg) marrow
4 tablespoons olive oil
2–4 cloves garlic, sliced
salt
freshly ground black pepper
2 teaspoons chopped sage
1 tablespoon chopped parsley
½ cup vegetable stock
butter
3 tablespoons wholemeal breadcrumbs
2 tablespoons grated parmesan *or* cheddar cheese

Preheat the oven to gas mark 6, 400°F (200°C). Peel the marrow, remove the seeds and cut into small chunks. Heat the oil in a heavy pan and gently fry the garlic for 2 minutes. Add the marrow and turn in the oil for 3 minutes. Season with salt and pepper to taste and add the herbs and stock. Cook together for 3 minutes then tip into a well-buttered ovenproof dish. Mix together the breadcrumbs and cheese and spread over the marrow mixture. Trail over 2–3 tablespoons of melted butter and bake in the oven until the top is crisp and golden (about 30 minutes).

Mushrooms

As in all country cookery, wild fare is a welcome addition to the pot. If you are able carefully to identify wild edible mushrooms, by all means substitute them in any of the following dishes.

Mushroom Omelette
(*Omelette aux Champignons*)

Serves 2

4 eggs
salt
freshly ground black pepper

For the filling:
1 oz (30 g) butter
4 oz (110 g) small mushrooms, sliced
freshly ground black pepper
pinch of finely chopped herbs
2 tablespoons natural yogurt *or* fromage frais

butter for cooking the omelette

Beat the eggs with the salt and pepper to taste in a bowl. Keep on one side. Make the filling by melting the butter in a small pan and gently frying the mushrooms until tender. Sprinkle with pepper while they are cooking. Stir in the herbs and yogurt and cook together for 2 minutes. Keep warm.

Put some melted butter in a hot omelette pan. Pour off the excess. Add the egg mixture and allow to solidify on the bottom of the pan. While the mixture is still liquid on the top, add the mushroom mixture. Cook the omelette until it solidifies a little more. Slide the slice under the omelette and tip out onto a plate.

Mushrooms Provence-Style
(*Champignons à la Provençale*)

Serves 4

4 tablespoons olive oil
1 lb (450 g) mushrooms, sliced
salt
freshly ground black pepper
2–4 cloves garlic, finely chopped
a few sage leaves
1 teaspoon chopped basil
1 teaspoon chopped oregano
3 tablespoons wholemeal breadcrumbs
lemon juice
black olives
1 tablespoon chopped parsley

Heat the oil in a heavy pan and gently fry the mushrooms for 2 minutes. Season with salt and pepper to taste. Add the garlic and herbs and fry together for 3 minutes. Add the breadcrumbs and fry together for a further 3 minutes. Put on a serving dish and sprinkle with lemon juice. Garnish with olives and parsley.

Mushrooms with Cream Sauce
(*Champignons à la Crème*)

Serves 4

2 tablespoons olive oil
2 tablespoons melted butter
1 bunch of spring onions, sliced
12 oz (350 g) small mushrooms, sliced
1–2 cloves garlic, crushed
salt
freshly ground black pepper
$\frac{1}{2}$ cup thick cream
$\frac{1}{2}$ cup natural yogurt *or* fromage frais
1 tablespoon chopped parsley

Heat the oil and butter in a heavy pan and gently fry the onions for 2 minutes. Add the mushrooms, garlic and salt and pepper to taste. Fry together for 3 minutes. Stir in the cream and yogurt and allow to heat through. Do not allow the dish to boil. Serve garnished with the chopped parsely.

Mushroom Pancakes
(Crêpes aux Champignons)

For the pancakes:
5 oz (150 g wholemeal flour
pinch of salt
12fl oz (350 ml) liquid ($\frac{1}{2}$ milk, $\frac{1}{2}$ water)
3 eggs
2 tablespoons melted butter *or* olive oil
oil for frying

For the filling:
12 oz (350 g) mushrooms, chopped
2 oz (60 g) butter
juice of $\frac{1}{2}$ lemon
salt
freshly ground black pepper
pinch of freshly grated nutmeg

For the white sauce:
1 pint (570 ml) milk
1 tablespoon sliced onion
1 bay leaf
1 teaspoon peppercorns
pinch of freshly grated nutmeg
3 oz (85 g) butter
2 oz (60 g) wholemeal flour

6 tablespoons milk
6 tablespoons cream *or* natural yogurt
3 oz (85 g) grated gruyère *or* cheddar cheese

First make the crêpes. Sift the flour and salt into a mixing bowl. Keep any bran in the sieve for adding to cereals or a bread mixture. Make a well in the centre of the flour and add half of the liquid. Gradually whisk together until a smooth batter is formed. Whisk in the eggs. Do not overbeat since this will make the crêpes tough. Stir in the melted butter and half of the remaining liquid. Cover the bowl with a cloth and allow to stand for 1–2 hours. Just before the batter is required, stir in enough of the remaining liquid to make a batter like thin cream.

Brush a 7-inch (18-cm) frying pan with oil and heat the pan gently until it begins to smoke. Spoon in enough batter to coat the bottom of the pan (2–3 tablespoons). Cook over a moderate heat until both sides are golden. Turn out onto a plate and keep warm. Continue making crêpes in the same way until all the batter is used up.

Put the mushrooms, 1 oz (30 g) of the butter, the lemon juice, salt and pepper to taste and 2 tablespoons of water into a saucepan. Cook together for a few minutes until the mushrooms are tender. Remove from the heat. Stir in the nutmeg.

Make the white sauce by bringing the milk just to the boil. Add the onion, bayleaf and peppercorns. Cover and allow to stand for 5 minutes. Melt the butter in a heavy pan and beat in the flour. Cook together over a gentle heat, beating continually with a fork or whisk for 2 minutes. Allow to cool. Strain the seasoned milk and pour onto the flour mixture, beating continuously. Bring to the boil then remove from the heat.

Stir half the sauce into the mushrooms. Spoon a tablespoon of mushroom mixture onto the centre of each crêpe and roll up. Arrange on a greased ovenproof dish. Stir the milk and cream into the remaining sauce. Reheat and pour over the crêpes. Sprinkle with grated cheese. Melt the remaining butter and sprinkle over the cheese. Brown under the grill and serve hot.

Mushrooms with Peppers
(*Champignons aux Poivrons*)

Serves 4

2 tablespoons olive oil
2 tablespoons melted butter
1 onion, finely chopped
1 green pepper, seeded and chopped, *or* 2 small peppers
1 lb (450 g) button mushrooms
8 oz (225 g) tomatoes, chopped in small pieces
salt
freshly ground black pepper
1 teaspoon paprika powder
2 teaspoons chopped parsley
$\frac{1}{2}$ cup dry red wine
2 tablespoons natural yogurt *or* fromage frais

Heat the oil and butter in a heavy pan and gently fry the onion until just golden. Add the pepper, mushrooms and tomatoes and turn in the oil for 3 minutes. Season to taste and add the paprika and parsley. Stir together for 5 minutes. Add the wine and yogurt and cook together for 5 minutes.

Stewed Mushrooms
(*Ragoût de Champignons*)

Serves 4

4 tablespoons olive oil
2 cloves garlic, finely chopped
1 tablespoon chopped parsley
1 lb (450 g) small mushrooms, sliced
1 cup stock
½ cup dry red wine
salt
freshly ground black pepper
2 teaspoons chopped tarragon

Heat the oil in a heavy pan and fry the garlic and parsley together for 2 minutes. Add the mushrooms and turn in the oil for 2 minutes. Add the stock, wine and salt and pepper to taste. Cover and stew together for 5 minutes. Serve garnished with the chopped herb.

Mushroom and Walnut Salad
(*Salade de Champignons aux Noix*)

Serves 4

This is an adaptation of a simple country recipe which uses truffles and walnuts, known as *Truffes et Cerneaux*. But both truffles and fresh walnuts are hard to come by in Britain. The truffle season opens in September and reaches its peak by mid-October. This coincides with the harvest of fresh walnuts.

4 oz (110 g) mushrooms *or* 4 black truffles
4 small lettuce hearts
walnut *or* hazelnut oil
wine vinegar
salt
freshly ground white pepper
16 fresh *or* mature walnuts

Finely slice the mushrooms or truffles and put in a serving bowl. Mix with the lettuce hearts and trickle over a little oil and vinegar. Sprinkle with salt and pepper. Scoop the fresh nuts from their shells or break mature nuts in halves. Stir into the mushroom and lettuce mixture. This salad is traditionally eaten with fresh bread and a light wine.

Onions

Onion Soup (*Soupe à l'Oignon*)   Serves 4

3 lb (1.35 kg) onions
3 oz (85 g) butter
1 teaspoon soft brown sugar
2 pints (1.14 litres) vegetable stock
salt
freshly ground black pepper
4 thick slices French bread
4 oz (110 g) grated gruyère *or* cheddar cheese

Put one onion on one side and slice the rest. Put half of the
butter in a soup pan and fry the sliced onions over a gentle heat
until they begin to turn golden. Do not allow them to burn. Peel
the whole onion and cut a slice off the top and bottom. Dip the
sliced ends in sugar. Melt a tablespoon of butter in a small
saucepan and cook the whole onion over a gentle heat until the
sugar caramelizes. Tip the onion and any melted butter into the
soup pan. Add the stock, salt and pepper to taste. Bring to the
boil and simmer for 10 minutes. Discard the whole onion.

Just before serving, lightly toast the bread slices and put into
four ovenproof bowls. Pour in the soup and sprinkle with a
good layer of cheese. Melt the remaining butter and trickle over
each bowl. Put the bowls under the grill and brown the cheese.
Serve hot.

Onion Flan (*Quiche aux Oignons*) Serves 4

For the pastry:
4 oz (110 g) wholemeal self-raising flour *or* 4 oz (110 g)
    wholemeal flour and 1 teaspoon baking powder
pinch of salt
1 oz (25 g) butter, cut in pieces
1 oz (25 g) margarine, cut in pieces
1 teaspoon soft brown sugar
3 tablespoons cold water
1 tablespoon olive oil

For the filling:
3 tablespoons olive oil
1 tablespoon melted butter
4 small onions, thinly sliced
salt
freshly ground black pepper
2 eggs
3 tablespoons thick cream *or* natural yogurt

First make the flan pastry. Sift the flour with the salt in a mixing bowl. Add the chilled fat with a knife and stir into the flour. Make into crumbs with the fingertips. In a separate bowl dissolve the sugar in the water and stir in the oil. Gradually add this mixture to the flour until a soft, pliable dough is formed which comes away from the sides of the bowl. You may not need all of the liquid. Use flour to make into a ball. Wrap in polythene and put in the refrigerator or a cool place for 20 minutes. After 10 minutes preheat the oven to gas mark 6, 400°F (200°C).

Meanwhile make the filling. Heat the oil and butter in a heavy pan and gently fry the onion until transparent. Season with salt and pepper to taste. Fry together until the onions are golden. Remove from the heat. Beat the eggs and cream together in a bowl.

Roll out the pastry on a floured board and place in a greased 8–9-inch (20–23-cm) flan tin with a removable base. Pull the pastry up the sides of the tin. Prick all over with a fork. Bake in the oven until the pastry has set (5–7 minutes). Allow to cool for a few minutes.

Arrange the onions in the flan base and spread over. Spoon in the egg mixture to fill in any gaps and to just cover the onions. Bake in the oven for 30 minutes. Allow to cool for a few minutes before removing from the tin. Serve hot or cold.

Onion Fritters (*Beignets d'Oignons*)   Serves 4

2 oz (60 g) wholemeal flour
pinch of salt
2 teaspoons olive oil
1 egg white
1 lb (450 g) onions
freshly ground black pepper
oil for deep-frying
lemon slices
2 teaspoons chopped parsley

To make the batter, sift the flour and salt together in a bowl. Make a well in the centre and pour in the oil and 3 tablespoons of tepid water. Gradually mix with the flour until a smooth creamy batter is formed, adding another 2 or 3 tablespoons of water as necessary. Leave on one side for 30 minutes. Just before the batter is required, beat the egg white well and fold into the batter. Mix well.

Meanwhile peel and trim the onions and slice. Put on a plate and sprinkle with salt and pepper. When the batter is ready, heat the oil in a heavy pan. Bring the batter near to the heat. When the oil is hot, put all the onion slices into the batter. Mix well and fry the slices in hot oil until golden. Allow to drain on absorbent paper and arrange on a serving dish with slices of lemon. Garnish with the chopped parsley.

Onions in Sweet and Sour Sauce   Serves 4
(*Confiture d'Oignons*)

This is typical of a new generation of tastes and textures pioneered by such celebrated chefs as Michel Guérard. Once you have appreciated the blend of vegetable, fruit and sugar, you are ready to begin your own experiments in combination. Like all the new dishes, delicate presentation is important.

4 oz (110 g) butter
1½ lb (675 g) small onions, thinly sliced
5–6 oz (140–170 g) caster sugar
1 teaspoon salt
½ teaspoon freshly ground black pepper
3 tablespoons sherry
3 tablespoons wine vinegar
2–3 dried apricots
2 glasses red wine

Gently heat the butter in a saucepan until it just begins to brown. Add the onions, sugar, and salt and pepper. Cover and allow to cook over a very low heat for 30 minutes, stirring from time to time. Add the sherry, vinegar, apricots and wine. Leave the lid off and cook for a further 30 minutes over a gentle heat.

Onion Gratin (*Gratin d'Oignons*)   Serves 4

2 tablespoons olive oil
2 tablespoons melted butter
12 oz (350 g) onions, chopped
2–4 cloves garlic, finely chopped
6 oz (170 g) mushrooms, sliced
salt
freshly ground black pepper
1 tablespoon chopped parsley
1 teaspoon chopped oregano
½ cup fromage frais *or* natural yogurt
3 tablespoons wholemeal breadcrumbs
freshly grated nutmeg

Preheat the oven to gas mark 5, 375°F (190°C). Heat the oil and butter in a heavy pan and fry the onions over a gentle heat for 5 minutes. Add the garlic and fry for 2 minutes. Add the mushrooms and season with salt and pepper to taste. Turn in the oil for 3 minutes. Add the herbs and fromage frais and cook together for 5 minutes. Turn into a well-greased ovenproof dish and cover with the breadcrumbs. Sprinkle with nutmeg and bake in the oven until the top is golden (about 30 minutes).

Onion Omelette (*Omelette aux Oignons*)   Makes 1

At harvest time (*moissons*) in the Midi, part of the work contract was five meals a day. At 1 pm the harvest worker would be given a bowl of soup and a thick onion omelette with some bread.

3 tablespoons melted butter
1 onion, sliced
salt
freshly ground black pepper
2 teaspoons chopped herbs
2 eggs, beaten

Heat the butter in an omelette pan and gently fry the onions until just golden. Season with salt and pepper to taste. In a separate bowl, beat the herbs with the eggs. Pour in the fried onions, leaving a coating of butter in the frying pan. Turn up the heat a little and add the onion and egg mixture. Allow it to spread over the bottom of the pan. Slip out onto a plate just before the omelette is completely set.

Stewed Onions (*Ragoût d'Oignons*)   Serves 4

3 tablespoons olive oil
1 tablespoon melted butter
1 lb (450 g) small onions, thickly sliced
1–2 cloves garlic, sliced
salt
freshly ground black pepper
8 oz (225 g) tomatoes, chopped
1 teaspoon chopped thyme
1 teaspoon chopped basil
1 tablespoon chopped parsley
$\frac{1}{2}$ cup vegetable stock
1 cup dry wine

Heat the oil and butter in a heavy pan and gently fry the onions until transparent. Add the garlic and season with salt and pepper to taste. Add the tomatoes and herbs and turn in the oil for 3 minutes. Add the stock and wine. Cover and allow to stew for 20 minutes.

Parsnips

Parsnip Patties
(*Croquettes de Panais*)

Serves 4

1 lb (450 g) parsnips
salt
2 tablespoons melted butter
freshly ground black pepper
pinch of freshly grated nutmeg
wholemeal flour
1 egg, beaten
wholemeal breadcrumbs
oil for frying
lemon wedges
sprig of parsley

Peel and trim the parsnips and slice. Boil in slightly salted water until tender. Drain and mash. Season with salt, pepper and nutmeg. Add a little flour to make a lump which can easily be divided into 12 balls. Roll each ball in flour and flatten a little with the hands. Leave on one side for 20 minutes. Dip each croquette first in beaten egg then roll in breadcrumbs. Fry in hot oil until golden on both sides. Put on a serving dish with lemon wedges. Garnish with parsley.

This recipe could be used with other roots such as carrot, swede or turnip.

Parsnip Loaf (*Pain au Panais*)   Serves 4–6

1½ lb (675 g) parsnips
salt
2 tablespoons olive oil
1 small onion, sliced
2 oz (60 g) wholemeal flour
freshly ground black pepper
3 eggs
2 tablespoons milk *or* cream *or* yogurt
butter

Peel and trim the parsnips and slice. Boil in slightly salted water until tender. Preheat the oven to gas mark 6, 400°F (200°C). Drain the parsnips and mash. Heat the olive oil in a frying pan and fry the onion until just golden. Mix in the mashed parsnip and heat through. Remove from the heat. In a mixing bowl, combine the flour with a little salt and pepper, the eggs, milk and a tablespoon of melted butter. Gradually beat together and leave to stand for 30 minutes. Mix in the parsnip mixture. Put into a well-buttered ovenproof dish and bake in the oven until the loaf is firm (30–40 minutes).

The loaf may be served with a sauce of your choice.

Peas

Pea Soup (*Potage St. Germain*)   Serves 4

1¼ pints (840 ml) vegetable stock
3 sprigs fresh mint
10 oz (285 g) fresh *or* frozen peas
salt
freshly ground black pepper
5 fl oz (150 ml) single cream *or* natural yogurt
1 teaspoon soft brown sugar
1 oz (30 g) butter, cut into small pieces

Put the stock, 2 mint sprigs, peas and salt and pepper to taste in
a heavy soup pan and simmer together until the peas are
tender. Discard the mint sprigs. Purée the soup in a blender or
liquidizer. Stir in half the cream and the sugar and gently heat
the soup. Do not allow to boil. Stir in the butter. Meanwhile,
finely chop the third mint sprig.

    Pour the soup into separate bowls. Add a spoonful of cream
to each helping and garnish with a little chopped mint.

Peas with Lettuce and Cream Sauce   Serves 6
(*Petits Pois à la Française*)

2 oz (60 g) butter
2 lb (900 g) par-cooked fresh peas *or* frozen peas
1 lettuce, trimmed and quartered
1 bunch spring onions, trimmed and thickly sliced
1 teaspoon chopped mint
1 teaspoon chopped parsley
salt
freshly ground black pepper

1 teaspoon soft brown sugar
2 tablespoons cream
2 tablespoons natural yogurt *or* fromage frais

Heat the butter in a heavy pan and add the peas, lettuce, onions and herbs. Turn in the hot butter for 3 minutes. Season with salt and pepper to taste. Add the sugar. Cover and cook over a very low heat for 10 minutes. Stir in the cream and yogurt and allow to heat through. Do not allow the dish to boil.

Broad beans may also be prepared this way.

Peas with Onions   Serves 4–6
(*Petits Pois aux Oignons*)

2 lb (900 g) fresh peas
salt
2 tablespoons olive oil
2 tablespoons melted butter
1 onion, sliced
2 tablespoons wholemeal flour
1 tablespoon lemon juice
1 teaspoon soft brown sugar
freshly ground black pepper
1 tablespoon chopped parsley

Cook the peas in boiling slightly salted water until tender. Drain but retain the cooking liquid. Heat the oil and butter in a heavy pan and gently fry the onion until transparent. Raise the heat and allow to turn just golden. Lower the heat and gradually stir in the flour. Remove from the heat and gradually stir in 2 cups of pea water or equivalent amount of vegetable stock, stirring all the time. Heat again for 2 minutes. Add the lemon juice, sugar and peas. Season with salt and pepper to taste and cook together for 5 minutes. Serve sprinkled with chopped parsley.

Peasant's Peas
(*Petits Pois à la Paysanne*)

Typical of the country style, use whatever odds and ends of vegetables you have to hand.

2 tablespoons olive oil
2 tablespoons melted butter
1 onion, sliced
2 carrots, trimmed and sliced
2 potatoes, cut in small chunks
2–4 cloves garlic, finely chopped
12 oz (350 g) shelled peas
salt
freshly ground black pepper
1 teaspoon chopped sage
1 teaspoon chopped basil
2 teaspoons chopped parsley
2 tablespoons natural yogurt *or* fromage frais
½ cup dry wine
½ cup vegetable stock

Heat the oil and butter in a heavy pan and gently fry the onion until just golden. Add the carrots, potatoes, garlic and peas and turn in the oil for 3 minutes. Season with salt and pepper to taste and add the herbs. Cook together for 5 minutes. Add the yogurt, wine and stock. Cover and cook together until all the vegetables are tender.

Peppers

Pepper and Tomato Omelette
(*Omelette aux Poivron et Tomates*)

Serves 4–6

4 tablespoons olive oil
1 small onion, finely chopped
1 green pepper, seeded and chopped
8 oz (225 g) tomatoes, chopped
2–3 cloves garlic, finely chopped
2 teaspoons chopped basil
2 teaspoons chopped parsley
salt
freshly ground black pepper
6 eggs
butter

Heat the oil in a heavy pan and fry the onion until just golden. Add the pepper, tomatoes, garlic and herbs and turn in the oil for 5 minutes. Season with salt and pepper to taste. Beat the eggs together until well mixed. Put a heavy frying pan on a low heat and heat some butter. When the butter is melted, pour off the excess. Pour in the egg mixture. When the bottom of the omelette begins to solidify, add the pepper and tomato mixture. Continue cooking until the omelette is almost set. Turn out onto a plate and cut into portions.

Pepper and Rice Salad
(*Salade de Riz aux Poivrons*)

Serves 4

4 cups cooked rice
$\frac{1}{2}$ green pepper, seeded and chopped
$\frac{1}{2}$ red pepper, seeded and chopped
1 tablespoon chopped chives
1 tablespoon chopped parsley *or* basil
2 teaspoons chopped oregano
salt
freshly ground black pepper
1 tablespoon chopped tarragon
olive oil
wine vinegar

Put the rice into a salad bowl and mix in the peppers, chives, parsley and oregano. Season with salt and pepper to taste. Sprinkle with chopped tarragon. Serve with olive oil and vinegar so that a vinaigratte sauce can be made to taste.

Peppers and Scrambled Egg (*Piperade*)

Serves 2

This is one of the many versions of the classic Basque dish.

3 tablespoons olive oil
1 small onion, sliced
2 tomatoes, chopped
1 clove garlic, finely chopped
salt
freshly ground black pepper
1 red *or* green pepper, seeded and cut into small pieces
6 eggs, beaten

Heat the oil in a heavy pan. Add the onion and gently fry until transparent and soft. Add the tomatoes, garlic and salt and pepper to taste and cook over a gentle heat for 10 minutes. Stir in the pepper and cook for a further 5 minutes. Beat the eggs until frothy and stir them into the tomato mixture. Cook together on a low heat until the eggs are cooked but still moist. Serve hot.

Baked Peppers (*Poivrons au Four*)   Serves 4

1 green pepper
1 red pepper
1 onion
6 oz (170 g) mushrooms
1–2 cloves garlic, crushed
sprig of thyme
sprig of parsley
salt
freshly ground black pepper
3 tablespoons olive oil
1 tablespoon melted butter
3 tablespoons fromage frais *or* natural yogurt

Preheat the oven to gas mark 5, 375°F (190°C). Seed the peppers
and cut into slices. Trim the onion and slice. Slice the
mushrooms. Put the sliced vegetables in a well-greased
ovenproof dish. Add the garlic and herbs. Sprinkle over salt
and pepper to taste. Trail over the oil and melted butter and
spread with fromage frais. Bake in the oven until the peppers
are tender (35–45 minutes).

Potatoes

The 'earth-apple' was introduced into France as an ornamental plant around 1540. In 1630, cultivation of the potato was still banned for fear of leprosy and it was considered unfit for human consumption until 1771. However in 1773 Parmentier published his *Chemical Examination of Potato, Wheat and Rice* and from then on the potato gradually became more and more popular. It is now an important part of the French diet.

Potato and Bean Salad   Serves 4
(*Salade de Pommes de Terre et Haricots*)

10 oz (285 g) potatoes, cut in small pieces
10 oz (285 g) haricot beans
salt
1 tablespoon lemon juice
freshly ground black pepper
1 teaspoon French mustard
6 tablespoons olive oil
1 clove garlic, crushed
1 small cucumber, sliced
10 black olives, stoned and halved
3 medium tomatoes, cut in quarters

Boil the potatoes and beans in separate pans in slightly salted water until tender. Meanwhile make up the dressing. Whisk the lemon juice with a good pinch of salt and pepper and the mustard. Gradually whisk in the oil and garlic until the sauce is well blended. Put the cooked vegetables in a large salad bowl with the cucumber and mix together with the dressing. Arrange the olives over the top of the salad and the tomatoes around the edge of the bowl.

Potato and Cream Pie
(*Pâté Bourbonnais*)

Serves 4–6

For the pastry:
4 oz (110 g) wholemeal flour
4 oz (110 g) self-raising flour
pinch of salt
2 oz (60 g) margarine
2 oz (60 g) butter
cold water

For the filling:
1½ lb (675 g) par-cooked potatoes
1 small onion, chopped
2 tablespoons chopped parsley
2 cloves garlic, finely chopped
salt
freshly ground black pepper
1 oz (30 g) butter
5–7 fl oz (150-200 ml) thick cream *or* fromage frais

Make the pastry by sifting the flour and salt into a mixing bowl. Cut the fat into pieces and rub into the flour with the fingertips to make crumbs. Sprinkle over 2 tablespoons of water and squeeze into the flour. Gradually add a little water at a time until a smooth dough is formed. Make up into a ball and wrap in polythene. Put in the refrigerator for 30 minutes to rest.

Preheat the oven to gas mark 6, 400°F (200°C). In a bowl mix together the potatoes, onion, parsley, garlic with salt and pepper to taste. Grease a 9½-inch (24-cm) metal pie dish. Roll out two-thirds of the pastry on a floured board and line the pie dish. Put in the potato filling. Melt the butter and trickle over the mixture. Roll out the rest of the pastry to make a lid for the pie. Moisten the edge of the pastry lining and press on the lid. Press round the edge with a fork. Prick a few holes in the lid and bake in the oven until the crust is golden (about 30 minutes). Remove from the oven. Make a small hole in the centre of the pie lid. Carefully pour in the cream. Serve hot or cold.

Potato Soup (*Potage des Vendanges*)   Serves 4

Les vendanges is the grape harvest. This nourishing soup is typical of those served to grape pickers during this season of hard work.

3 tablespoons melted butter
2 leeks, trimmed, washed and chopped
1 lb (450 g) potatoes, cut in pieces
2½ pints (1.43 litres) vegetable stock
1 bay leaf
1 tablespoon chopped parsley
salt
freshly ground black pepper
1 cup soft white cheese *or* fromage frais
1 tablespoon chopped tarragon

Heat the butter in a heavy pan and cook the leeks until they soften. Add the potatoes and turn in the butter for 3 minutes. Add the stock, herbs and salt and pepper to taste. Cook on a low heat until the potatoes are tender. Purée in a blender or liquidizer. Return to the pan and stir in the soft cheese. Serve garnished with chopped tarragon.

Potato Omelette (*Omelette Paysanne*)   Serves 2

2 tablespoons olive oil
1 small onion, finely chopped
4 oz (110 g) tomatoes, chopped
1 medium potato, cooked and diced
2 tablespoons finely chopped parsley *or* other fresh herb
4 eggs
salt
freshly ground black pepper
1 oz (30 g) butter

Heat the oil in a heavy frying pan and fry the onion until transparent. Add the tomatoes and potato and cook together until the potato begins to turn golden. Add the herbs and remove from the heat. Beat the eggs in a bowl with salt and pepper to taste. Heat the butter in an omelette pan and pour in the egg mixture. Stir well for 10 seconds with the flat of a fork until the eggs begin to solidify. Tip the pan so that any uncooked egg mixture can flow to the sides. Continue cooking until the eggs are almost set. Stir in the fried vegetables and stir for a few seconds. Cook for a further few seconds to brown the bottom of the omelette. The top should be almost firm. Remove from the heat. Put a plate over the top of the pan and tip out the omelette. Slide the omelette back into the pan to brown the other side. Tip out onto a serving plate and cut into wedges. Serve hot or cold.

Potatoes Midi-Style   Serves 4–6
(*Tian du Midi*)

Tian is a Provençal word for a thick cake-like dish. It may be fried in a pan or finished in the oven.

2 lb (900 g) potatoes
oil for frying
4 oz (110 g) onions, sliced
4 oz (110 g) grated parmesan *or* cheddar cheese
1 teaspoon chopped thyme
1 teaspoon chopped basil
1 teaspoon chopped oregano
1 teaspoon chopped parsley
salt
freshly ground black pepper
1 lb (450 g) tomatoes, sliced

Par-cook the potatoes in boiling water. Drain and peel. Allow to cool and slice. Preheat the oven to gas mark 5, 375°F (190°C). Heat a few tablespoons of oil in a heavy pan and fry the potato slices until just golden. Drain on absorbent paper. Put a layer of potato slices in the bottom of a greased ovenproof dish. Cover with a layer of onions. Sprinkle with cheese. Mix the herbs together and sprinkle some over the cheese. Add a pinch of salt and pepper. Cover with a layer of tomato slices. Put in a similar layer of potatoes, onions, cheese, herbs and tomatoes. When all the ingredients are used up, bake in the oven for 30 minutes.

Potato Gratin
(*Gratin Dauphinois*)

Serves 4

This is one of the classic dishes of France. It excels in simplicity of preparation and taste. Although many versions abound in France, the original is a nourishing mountain dish from the Alps of the Dauphiné.

2 lb (900 g) potatoes
1–2 cloves garlic, finely chopped
salt
freshly ground black pepper
1 pint (600 ml) double cream
1 oz (30 g) butter, cut in pieces

Preheat the oven to gas mark 2, 300°F (150°C). Peel the potatoes and slice as thinly as possible (old books mention 'gold pieces'). Layer into an earthenware gratin dish, sprinkling with garlic, salt and pepper as you put the potato slices in. Pour over the cream. Dot with pieces of butter. Cover loosely with foil. Put in the oven to bake for 1½ hours. Remove the foil and turn up the oven to gas mark 4, 350°F (180°C) to brown the top (about 10 minutes).

Potato and Cheese Cake
(*Galette de Pommes de Terre*)

Serves 4

1 lb (450 g) potatoes
salt
2 tablespoons melted butter
1 cup grated gruyère *or* cheddar cheese
freshly ground black pepper
freshly grated nutmeg
olive oil for frying
1 tablespoon chopped parsley
lemon wedges

Boil the potatoes in slightly salted water until soft. Drain and peel. In a bowl mash with the butter, cheese, pepper, nutmeg and a pinch of salt. Heat a few tablespoons of oil in a heavy frying pan and put in the potato mixture. Pat down with a slice to make a cake-like shape and allow to brown on the bottom.

Put a plate on the top and tip out onto the plate. Put the potato cake back in the pan the other way up to brown the other side. Add a little more oil if necessary. Serve garnished with parsley and lemon wedges.

Potatoes with Herbs
(*Pommes de Terre à la Paysanne*)   Serves 4

This dish reflects the country style of adding wild plants to a simple dish, bringing colour and extra nourishment at no extra cost.

1½ lb (675 g) potatoes
salt
2 tablespoons melted butter
2 tablespoons olive oil
1 onion, sliced
2 tablespoons wholemeal flour
1½ cups vegetable stock
½ cup dry wine
1–2 cloves garlic, finely chopped
a good handful of fresh herbs such as chervil, sorrel, dandelion,
   borage, parsley
freshly ground black pepper

Preheat the oven to gas mark 4, 350°F (180°C). Boil the potatoes in slightly salted water for 10 minutes. Drain and slice. Put in the bottom of a greased ovenproof dish. In a separate pan, heat the butter and oil and gently fry the onion until just golden. Stir in the flour and fry for 2 minutes. Gradually add the stock and wine. Stir together and pour over the potato slices. Put in the garlic. Scatter over the herbs and season with salt and pepper to taste. Mix together. Cover and bake in the oven for 1 hour. After 30 minutes remove the lid.

Pumpkins

Pumpkin Soufflé
(*Soufflé de Potiron*)

Serves 4–6

1 lb (450 g) pumpkin
salt
½ tablespoon wholemeal flour
15 fl oz (430 ml) milk
freshly ground black pepper
3 eggs
3 heaped tablespoons grated gruyère *or* cheddar cheese
1 teaspoon chopped herbs

Preheat the oven to gas mark 5, 375°F (190°C). Peel and seed the pumpkin and cut into small pieces. Put in a pan and just cover with water. Sprinkle on a pinch of salt and boil the pumpkin until soft. Drain well and mash. Press out any excess moisture. Put the flour in a cup and add a little milk. Stir together until there are no lumps. Heat the rest of the milk in a pan and pour in the flour mixture. Season with salt and pepper and heat gently until the milk thickens, stirring all the time. Allow to cool and whisk in the mashed pumpkin. Separate the egg yolks from the whites and whisk the yolks into the pumpkin mixture. Stir in the cheese and herbs. When the mixture is cold, beat the egg whites until stiff and fold into the pumpkin mixture. Pour the mixture into a well-buttered soufflé or ovenproof dish and bake in the oven until the mixture has risen and turned golden (about 30 minutes). Serve immediately.

Pumpkin Pancakes
(*Galettes de Potiron*)

12 oz (350 g) pumpkin piece
milk
2 eggs, beaten
2 teaspoons olive oil
pinch of salt
6 oz (170 g) wholemeal flour
oil for frying
lemon wedges

Peel and seed the pumpkin piece and cut into small chunks. Boil in water until soft. Purée in a blender or liquidizer. Add enough milk to make up to 1 pint (570 ml) of liquid. Beat in the eggs, oil and salt until well blended. Gradually stir in the flour until a smooth batter is obtained. Allow the batter to stand for 30 minutes before use. Heat a little oil in a heavy frying pan. Pour off the excess. Pour in enough batter to cover the bottom of the pan. Allow it to cook for 2–3 minutes then turn over and cook on the other side. Turn out onto a plate. Keep warm and serve with lemon wedges.

Butter may also be used for the frying. Take care not to let it burn.

Pumpkin Gratin (*Gratin de Potiron*)   Serves 4

2 lb (900 g) pumpkin
6 cloves garlic, finely chopped
4 tablespoons chopped parsley
1 teaspoon chopped thyme
1 teaspoon chopped mint
salt
freshly ground black pepper
4 tablespoons wholemeal flour
2 tablespoons natural yogurt *or* fromage frais
4 tablespoons olive oil
3 tablespoons wholemeal breadcrumbs

Preheat the oven to gas mark 4, 350°F (180°C). Peel the pumpkin and seed. Cut into very small pieces. On a plate, mix together the garlic, herbs, salt and pepper to taste and flour. Roll the pumpkin pieces in this mixture and put them in a well-greased ovenproof dish. Spread over the yogurt and trickle over 3 tablespoons of oil. Cover with the breadcrumbs and trickle over the rest of the oil. Bake in the oven for about 1 hour until the top is golden and the pumpkin pieces are tender.

Pumpkin Soup (*Soupe au Potiron*)   Serves 4

2 oz (60 g) butter
½ onion, finely chopped
1 lb (450 g) piece pumpkin
2 cloves garlic, finely chopped
salt
freshly ground black pepper
2 teaspoons chopped basil
2 teaspoons chopped parsley
2½ pints (1.43 litres) stock
4 tablespoons wholemeal breadcrumbs
1 tablespoon olive oil

Heat the butter in a heavy soup pan and gently fry the onion until transparent. Peel the pumpkin and cut in small pieces. Add to the onion with the garlic. Season with salt and pepper to taste. Turn in the hot butter for 4 minutes. Add the herbs and stock. Cover and simmer until the pumpkin is tender. Purée the soup in a blender or liquidizer. Fry the breadcrumbs in oil until golden. Stir into the soup. Serve hot.

Salsify

Vegetable Terrine with Salsify
(*Terrine de Légumes aux Salsifis*)

Serves 4

Here is a way of serving this unusual root vegetable with an easily prepared terrine.

4 tablespoons olive oil
12 oz (350 g) aubergine, cut into small pieces
8 oz (225 g) mushrooms, chopped
4 oz (110 g) carrots, peeled and chopped
8 oz (225 g) fresh spinach
2 eggs
salt
freshly ground black pepper
freshly grated nutmeg
26 oz (750 g) fresh salsify
lemon juice
1 tablespoon flour

Preheat the oven to gas mark 4, 350°F (180°C). Line a 1 lb (450 g) bread tin with greaseproof paper. Heat the oil in a heavy pan and gently fry the aubergine, mushrooms and carrots until the vegetables are tender (about 10 minutes). Meanwhile tear the spinach leaves in pieces and steam them for 10 minutes. Press out as much juice as possible and chop. Put all the fried vegetables in a bowl and mash together or put in a food processor and blend. Add the eggs and seasoning to taste and blend again.

Put one third of this mixture in the bottom of the tin. Add the spinach and spread out evenly. Put in the rest of the fried vegetable mixture and smooth out. Lightly rest a piece of greaseproof paper on the top and bake in the oven until the

137

terrine is firm and just beginning to shrink away from the sides of the tin (35–40 minutes). Remove from the oven and allow to cool then refrigerate for at least 2 hours.

Meanwhile prepare the salsify. Wash and peel with a potato-peeler, holding the roots flat on the table. Cut them into short (2 inch/5 cm) lengths and put in a bowl of water. Add a few drops of lemon juice to prevent the salsify from discolouring. Fill a saucepan with 1¾ pints (1 litre) of water into which a tablespoon of flour has been whisked. Season with a little lemon juice and salt. Bring to a gentle boil. Drain the salify and add to the flour liquid (*blanc*). Allow to cook over a gentle heat for 45 minutes. Allow to cool in the blanc. Drain when required.

Serve slices of cooled terrine with salsify or a sauce if salsify is unavailable.

Spinach

Baked Spinach (*Épinards au Four*)   Serves 4

1½ lb (675 g) spinach
2 tablespoons olive oil
1 tablespoon melted butter
1 small onion, finely chopped
6 oz (170 g) tomatoes, chopped
1–2 cloves garlic, finely chopped
salt
freshly ground black pepper
1 tablespoon chopped parsley
1 teaspoon chopped thyme
1 teaspoon chopped sage
2 tablespoons wholemeal flour
3 eggs, beaten
1 egg yolk
6 fl oz (170 ml) milk

Preheat the oven to gas mark 6, 400°F (200°C). Wash the spinach and blanch in boiling water for 3 minutes. Drain thoroughly and chop. Heat the oil and butter in a heavy pan and gently fry the onion until transparent. Add the tomatoes, garlic, salt and pepper to taste and turn in the oil for 3 minutes. Add the spinach and herbs and mix well over a gentle heat for a few minutes. Remove from the heat. In a separate bowl, beat the flour into the eggs and egg yolk. Stir in the milk. Pour into the spinach mixture. Put the mixture in a greased ovenproof dish and bake in the oven until the eggs are set and the top is a little golden in colour (30–40 minutes). Allow to cool for a few minutes before serving.

Spinach Soufflé
(*Soufflé aux Épinards*)

Serves 4

6 oz (170 g) spinach
salt
butter
4 tablespoons grated parmesan, gruyère *or* cheddar cheese
1 tablespoon chopped spring onion
2 tablespoons wholemeal flour
½ pint (285 ml) boiling milk
freshly ground black pepper
pinch of freshly grated nutmeg
4 egg yolks
5 egg whites

Preheat the oven to gas mark 6, 400°F (200°C). Blanch the spinach in slightly salted boiling water for 4 minutes. Drain well and chop. Butter a soufflé dish (2½-pint (1.43 litres) and sprinkle with 1 tablespoon of the grated cheese. Heat a tablespoon of butter in a pan and gently fry the spring onion for 1 minute. Add the spinach and a pinch of salt and cook until most of the spinach moisture has been driven off. Remove from the heat.

Prepare the soufflé sauce base by melting 2 oz (60 g) of butter in a heavy saucepan. Stir in the flour with a wooden spoon and stir with the butter for 2 minutes. Remove from the heat. When the mixture has stopped foaming, pour in the boiling milk. Beat well with a whisk until blended. Whisk in a pinch of salt, pepper and nutmeg. Put back on a moderate heat and stir together until the sauce thickens (about 1–2 minutes). Stir in the egg yolks and remove from the heat. Stir in the spinach mixture.

Beat the egg whites with a whisk until stiff. Stir a quarter of the egg white into the sauce base. Stir in 2 tablespoons of the grated cheese. Fold in the rest of the egg white and turn the mixture into the soufflé dish. Sprinkle with the last tablespoon of cheese and put into the oven. Turn down the heat to gas mark 5, 375°F (190°C) and bake until the soufflé has turned golden and risen well (25–30 minutes).

Spinach Patties
(*Petits Pâtés d'Épinards*)

Makes 6

1½ lb (675 g) spinach
4 cloves garlic, finely chopped
½ teaspoon salt
freshly ground black pepper
freshly grated nutmeg
wholemeal flour
oil for deep-frying
lemon slices

Wash the spinach, remove any coarse stalks and chop. Blanch in 2 cups of boiling water for 3 minutes. Drain thoroughly. Puree in a blender or liquidizer. Put into a bowl and add the garlic, salt, pepper, nutmeg and enough flour to make a firm mixture. Roll into 6 large balls, flatten slightly with the fingers and make into patties with the aid of a little flour. Fry in oil until golden on both sides. Drain on absorbent paper. Serve with lemon slices.

Spinach Gratin (*Gratin d'Épinards*)

Serves 4

1½ lb (675 g) spinach
2 tablespoons melted butter
1 small onion, sliced
salt
freshly grated nutmeg
freshly ground black pepper
3 tablespoons fromage frais *or* natural yogurt
2 tablespoons wholemeal breadcrumbs
2 tablespoons grated parmesan, gruyère *or* cheddar cheese

Preheat the oven to gas mark 6, 400°F (200°C). Blanch the spinach in boiling water for 3 minutes. Drain thoroughly and chop. Heat the butter in a heavy pan and fry the onion until just golden. Add the spinach and seasonings and turn in the hot butter for 3 minutes. Put in a greased ovenproof dish and spread with the fromage frais. Mix the breadcrumbs with the grated cheese and spread over the fromage frais. Bake in the oven until the top is crisp and golden (about 30 minutes).

Spinach with Poached Eggs
(*Oeufs Pochés Florentine*)

Serves 4 *or*
8 as a starter

Recipes with the word *florentine* traditionally contain spinach, which was thought to have been introduced into the French cuisine from Florence by Catherine de Medici.

2½ lb (1.12 kg) fresh spinach

For the white sauce:
16 fl oz (450 ml) milk
2 slices onion
1 bay leaf
6 peppercorns
1 oz (30 g) butter
2 tablespoons wholemeal flour

8 eggs
1 oz (30 g) butter
salt
freshly ground black pepper
freshly grated nutmeg
2 egg yolks
3 oz (85 g) grated gruyère *or* cheddar cheese
1 teaspoon French mustard
4 tablespoons milk

Blanch the spinach in boiling water for 4 minutes, drain thoroughly and chop. Keep warm.

Make the white sauce by bringing the milk to the boil. Remove from the heat. Add the onion, bay leaf and peppercorns. Cover and allow to stand for 5 minutes. Heat the butter in a heavy saucepan and whisk in the flour. Whisk together over a gentle heat for 2 minutes. Strain the aromatized milk onto this mixture, whisking continuously. Bring the sauce to the boil and remove from the heat. Meanwhile poach the eggs.

Melt 1 oz (30 g) butter and stir into the warm spinach. Stir in salt, pepper and nutmeg to taste. Spread over the bottom of a greased ovenproof dish. Turn on the grill to preheat. Drain the poached eggs and arrange on the spinach. Beat the egg yolks, 2 oz (60 g) of the cheese and the mustard into the white sauce. The sauce should thickly coat the spoon. If it is too thick, stir in a little milk. Spoon the sauce over the eggs and spinach. Sprinkle with the rest of the cheese and brown under the grill. Serve hot.

Spinach with Cream
(*Epinards à la Crème*)

Serves 4

2 lb (900 g) spinach
salt
2 oz (60 g) butter
freshly ground black pepper
freshly grated nutmeg
1 cup thick cream *or* fromage frais

Blanch the spinach in slightly salted boiling water for 5 minutes. Drain well and chop. Heat the butter in a heavy pan and add the spinach. Season with pepper and nutmeg and turn the spinach in the hot butter. Stir in the cream. When the cream is well blended, serve the spinach with garlic-flavoured warm bread.

Sweetcorn

Grilled Sweetcorn with Tarragon Butter   Serves 4
(*Epis de Maïs Grillé au Beurre d'Estragon*)

1 glass dry white wine
2 teaspoons fresh tarragon leaves
8 oz (225 g) butter, softened
salt
freshly ground black pepper
4 cobs sweetcorn

The tarragon butter may be made in advance or just before the
sweetcorn is grilled. Put the wine and herbs in a small saucepan
and bring to the boil. Lower the heat and allow to reduce until
about 3 tablespoons of liquid remain. Allow to cool for a few
minutes. Add the softened butter and salt and pepper to taste.
Mix together with a small whisk or fork to make a smooth thick
cream. Keep on one side.

Trim off the leaves of the sweetcorn and cook the cobs in
plenty of boiling water for 5 minutes. Drain. Spread with a little
of the tarragon butter and cook under the grill until golden (15–
20 minutes), turning the cobs so that they are evenly grilled.
Serve with the rest of the tarragon butter.

Naturally this method lends itself to barbecue cooking or
cooking on a spit.

Sweetcorn Salad (*Salade de Maïs*)   Serves 4

12–14 oz (340 g) tinned *or* frozen sweetcorn
knob of butter
salt
freshly ground black pepper
a few fresh tarragon leaves
1 small crisp lettuce
1 small green pepper, seeded and diced
2 small tomatoes, cut in pieces
1 apple, cored and cut in small pieces

Cook the sweetcorn in its juice or a small amount of water until it is well warmed through (5–7 minutes). Drain and stir in the butter, salt and pepper to taste, and tarragon. Keep warm.

Meanwhile prepare the rest of the salad. Arrange the lettuce around the edge of the salad bowl. Stir the green pepper, tomato and apple into the warm sweetcorn. Put this mixture in the middle of the lettuce leaves. Serve while still warm.

Swiss Chard

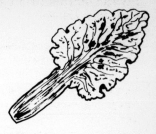

Swiss chard belongs to the same family as beetroot. It is widely cultivated in France, especially around the Lyons area. It is known by various names including *bette*, *blette* and *poirée à carde*.

Swiss Chard with Butter Sauce   Serves 4
(*Bettes au Beurre*)

The simplest way to prepare any green vegetable is to boil it until just tender (a few minutes only) and then to gently braise it in butter with a little seasoning.

1½ lb (675 g) Swiss chard leaves
salt
2 tablespoons melted butter
1 tablespoon chopped parsley
freshly ground black pepper

Wash the green leaves and strip the leaf from the stem. Blanch in a pan of boiling slightly salted water until tender (about 10 minutes). Drain thoroughly and slice. Heat the butter in a heavy pan and stir in the Swiss chard. Add the parsley and season lightly with a little pepper. Stir together for 2 minutes.

Swiss Chard with Eggs
(*Bettes en Gâteau*)

Serves 4

1½ lb (675 g) Swiss chard leaves
2 tablespoons olive oil
1 tablespoon melted butter
1 bunch spring onions, sliced
4 oz (110 g) mushrooms, sliced
salt
freshly ground black pepper
1 teaspoon chopped parsley
1 teaspoon chopped thyme
2 tablespoons wholemeal flour
3 eggs, beaten
1 egg yolk
6 fl oz (170 ml) milk

Preheat the oven to gas mark 6, 400°F (200°C). Wash the Swiss chard and strip the green leaf from the stems. Blanch the leaves in boiling water for 5 minutes. Drain thoroughly and chop. Heat the oil and butter in a heavy pan and fry the spring onion for 3 minutes. Add the mushrooms, salt and pepper to taste and turn in the oil for 3 minutes. Add the Swiss chard and herbs and mix well over a gentle heat for a few minutes. Remove from the heat. In a separate bowl, beat the flour into the eggs and egg yolk. Stir in the milk. Pour into the Swiss chard mixture. Put the mixture in a greased ovenproof dish and bake in the oven until the eggs are set and the top begins to turn golden (30–40 minutes). Allow to cool for a few minutes before serving.

Swiss Chard and Apple Pie
(*Tourte de Blea*)

This is a savoury variation of the classic Provençal dish.

For the pastry:
4 oz (110 g) wholemeal flour
4 oz (110 g) self-raising flour
2 oz (60 g) margarine
2 oz (60 g) butter
pinch of salt

For the filling:
10 oz (285 g) Swiss chard leaves
10 oz (285 g) cooking apples
2 tablespoons melted butter
½ onion, sliced
2 cloves garlic, finely chopped
1 cup cooked haricot beans
1 teaspoon chopped thyme
1 teaspoon chopped sage
1 teaspoon chopped basil
1 tablespoon pine nuts *or* sliced almonds
salt
freshly ground black pepper
milk for glazing

Make sure all the items for making the pastry are cool. Mix the flours together in a bowl. Cut the margarine and butter into pieces. Sift the flour with the salt and add the pieces of margarine and butter. Make into crumbs with the fingertips. Sprinkle 2 tablespoons of cold water over and cut into the flour mixture with a knife. Add a little more water to make a smooth dough which comes away cleanly from the sides of the bowl. Wrap in polythene and allow to rest in the refrigerator for 30 minutes.

Wash and trim the Swiss chard leaves and blanch in boiling water for 6 minutes. Drain thoroughly and chop. Peel and core the apples and cut into thin slices. Cook in a little water for 5 minutes. Drain. Heat the butter in a heavy pan and fry the onion until golden. Add the garlic and turn in the butter for 2 minutes. Add the Swiss chard, apples, beans, herbs, nuts and salt and pepper to taste. Cook together for 5 minutes. Preheat the oven to gas mark 6, 400°F (200°C).

Roll out the pastry with the help of a little dry flour. Use two-thirds of it to line the bottom and sides of a greased 9½-inch (24-cm) pie dish. Put in the filling ingredients. Cover with the pastry lid. This should be joined to the base by moistening with a little water and pressing the two edges together with a fork. Prick holes in the lid and brush with milk to glaze. Bake in the oven until golden (about 30 minutes).

Swiss Chard Gratin   Serves 4
(*Gratin de Bettes*)

1 lb (450 g) Swiss chard leaves
salt
freshly ground black pepper
8 oz (225 g) mushrooms, sliced
1 cup thick cream *or* fromage frais
freshly grated nutmeg
4 tablespoons grated gruyère *or* cheddar cheese

Preheat the oven to gas mark 5, 375°F (190°C). Wash and trim the Swiss chard leaves and blanch in boiling water for 5 minutes. Drain thoroughly and chop. Put half of the Swiss chard in the bottom of a greased ovenproof dish and season with a little salt and pepper. Put in the sliced mushrooms and cover with the rest of the Swiss chard. Season again. Pour over the cream and sprinkle with a little nutmeg. Cover with grated cheese and bake in the oven until the top is golden (30–40 minutes).

Tomatoes

Tomatoes are widely cultivated in France especially in the valley of the Garonne. The south produces the large tomato known as the Mediterranean tomato which is ideal for stuffing.

Tomato and Vegetable Soup
(Potage à la Liégeoise)

Serves 4

This is a nourishing soup typical of the industrial north.

2 tablespoons olive oil
2 tablespoons melted butter
1 onion, sliced
2 stalks celery, sliced
2 tablespoons chopped parsley
8 oz (225 g) tomatoes, chopped
8 oz (225 g) potatoes, chopped
handful of chopped fresh herbs
salt
freshly ground black pepper
1 teaspoon chopped sage
2 cloves garlic, crushed
2½ pints (1.43 litres) vegetable stock *or* water
1 tablespoon tomato purée

Heat the oil and butter in a heavy pan and fry the onion until just golden. Add the celery, parsley, tomatoes, potatoes, herbs and salt and pepper to taste. Fry together for 5 minutes. Add the sage and garlic and turn in the oil. Add the stock and tomato purée and stir together. Cover and cook over a gentle heat for 30 minutes. Serve with fried or warmed crusty bread.

Tomato Salad (*Salade de Tomates*)   Serves 4

1 lb (450 g) tomatoes, sliced
4 oz (110 g) spring onions, sliced
1 tablespoon wine vinegar
1 teaspoon soft brown sugar
salt
freshly ground black pepper
$\frac{1}{2}$ teaspoon French mustard
3 tablespoons olive oil
$\frac{1}{2}$–1 clove garlic, finely chopped
1 tablespoon chopped fresh basil *or* parsley

Arrange the tomatoes and onions on a serving dish. Whisk together the vinegar, sugar, a good pinch of salt and pepper and the mustard. Gradually whisk in the oil, garlic and herbs until the sauce is well blended. Spoon over the tomatoes and onions. Cover and leave to stand for 1 hour.

Tomato Soup (*Potage aux Tomates*)   Serves 4–6

2 tablespoons olive oil
2 tablespoons melted butter
1 small onion, finely chopped
2 lb (900 g) tomatoes, chopped
8 oz (225 g) potatoes, chopped
1 teaspoon salt
$\frac{1}{2}$ teaspoon freshly ground black pepper
1 teaspoon soft brown sugar
3 pints (1.75 litres) thin stock *or* water
1 tablespoon chopped parsley

Heat the oil and butter in a heavy soup pan and fry the onion until transparent. Add the tomatoes and potato and mix well with the oil. Sprinkle with salt, pepper and sugar. Add the stock and bring to the boil. Cover and turn down the heat to simmer until the vegetables are soft. Purée in a blender or liquidizer. Serve garnished with chopped parsley.

Stuffed Tomatoes (*Tomates Farcies*)   Serves 4

8 large tomatoes
4 tablespoons olive oil
1 onion, finely chopped
2–4 cloves garlic, finely chopped
2 cups cooked rice
1 cup chopped walnuts *or* almonds
1 cup wholemeal breadcrumbs
1 teaspoon salt
½ teaspoon freshly ground black pepper
2 teaspoons chopped basil
1 tablespoon chopped parsley

Preheat the oven to gas mark 5, 375°F (190°C). Wash the tomatoes and slice off the tops. Keep on one side. Scoop out the pulp and retain. Arrange the tomato shells on a greased baking dish. Heat the oil in a heavy pan and gently fry the onion for 3 minutes. Add the garlic, rice, nuts, breadcrumbs and tomato pulp. Sprinkle with salt, pepper and herbs. Mix together and fry for 5 minutes. Put some of the filling mixture in each of the tomato shells. Put the tops back on. Bake in the oven for 30 minutes.

Fried Tomatoes (*Tomates Provençales*)   Serves 4

8 tomatoes
4 tablespoons olive oil
salt
freshly ground black pepper
2 cloves garlic, finely chopped
3 tablespoons wholemeal breadcrumbs
1 teaspoon chopped sage
1 teaspoon chopped oregano
1 teaspoon chopped thyme
1 teaspoon chopped parsley

Cut the tomatoes in halves. Heat the oil in a heavy pan and gently fry the tomato halves. Sprinkle with a little salt and pepper. Cover the pan with a lid to prevent the oil spitting. Remove the tomatoes and keep warm. Put the garlic in the hot oil and fry for 2 minutes. Add the breadcrumbs and herbs. Fry together for 3 minutes. Sprinkle over the fried tomatoes. Serve hot.

Tomatoes with Mushrooms   Serves 4
(*Tomates au Four*)

4 tablespoons olive oil
1 lb (450 g) tomatoes, chopped
8 oz (225 g) mushrooms, sliced
2 cloves garlic, finely chopped
2 teaspoons chopped parsley
2 teaspoons chopped thyme
2 teaspoons chopped basil
salt
freshly ground black pepper
1 egg, beaten
4 tablespoons wholemeal breadcrumbs
2 tablespoons melted butter

Preheat the oven to gas mark 6, 400°F (200°C). Heat the oil in a heavy pan and fry the tomatoes for 3 minutes. Add the mushrooms, garlic, herbs and salt and pepper to taste. Fry together for 3 minutes and then add the beaten egg. Stir well and pour into a greased ovenproof dish. Cover with the breadcrumbs. Trickle over the melted butter and bake in the oven until the top is crisp and golden (15–20 minutes).

Tomato and Courgette Summer Soup Serves 4
(*Potage Glacé à la Catalane*)

The ancient province of Catalonia straddles the Pyrenees, having both French and Spanish regions. This cold soup, which has relatives across the border, is delicious during a hot spell.

1 lb (450 g) tomatoes, chopped
2 courgettes, sliced
3-inch (8-cm) piece cucumber, sliced
1 small onion, chopped
2 cloves garlic, sliced
1 stick celery, chopped
4 tablespoons olive oil
pinch of saffron
1 cup milk or natural yogurt
1½ pints (855 ml) vegetable stock
salt
freshly ground black pepper
pinch of cayenne pepper

Purée all the vegetables in a blender or liquidizer. Pour into a bowl. Stir in the oil. Dissolve the saffron in the milk. It should turn a nice yellow orange colour. Stir into the puréed vegetables. Add the stock and seasoning to taste. Stir well together and chill. Serve cold.

Turnip

The turnip is generally used in France as a pot vegetable like the carrot or onion. French cooks prefer the small white and purple turnip which has a mild, slightly sweet taste. The best turnips for this purpose are said to come from the area around Meaux.

Turnips with Cream Sauce   Serves 4
(*Navets à la Crème*)

1½ lb (675 g) turnips
salt
1 tablespoon butter
1 tablespoon wholemeal flour
5 fl oz (150 ml) milk
5 fl oz (150 ml) cream
freshly ground black pepper
1 tablespoon dry wine

Peel the turnips and cut into small chunks. Boil in a little slightly salted water until just tender. Drain and keep warm. Meanwhile make the cream sauce. Melt the butter in a heavy saucepan over a low heat. Stir in the flour and stir together for 2 minutes. Remove the roux from the heat. As soon as it has stopped bubbling, whisk in hot milk. Whisk well until it is well blended. Whisk in the cream. Season with salt and pepper and stir in the wine. Pour the cream sauce over the cooked turnips.

Turnip Stew (*Ragoût de Navets*)   Serves 4

1½ lb (675 g) turnips
salt
3 tablespoons olive oil
1 onion, finely chopped
1 tablespoon wholemeal flour
8 oz (225 g) tomatoes, chopped
2 cloves garlic, finely chopped
freshly ground black pepper
1 cup vegetable stock
1 teaspoon chopped sage
1 tablespoon chopped parsley

Peel the turnips and cut into small chunks. Blanch in boiling slightly salted water for 5 minutes. Drain. Heat the oil in a heavy pan and gently fry the onion until transparent. Stir in the flour and fry together for 2 minutes. Add the tomatoes, garlic and turnip and season with salt and pepper to taste. Stir together for 5 minutes. Add the stock and sage and cover. Cook over a low heat until the turnip is tender, adding more stock if necessary to prevent sticking. Serve garnished with the chopped parsley.

Turnip Gratin (*Gratin de Navets*)   Serves 4

1½ lb (675 g) turnips
salt
2 tablespoons melted butter
1 clove garlic, finely chopped
freshly ground black pepper
1 teaspoon chopped sage
1 teaspoon chopped parsley
1 teaspoon chopped chervil
4 tablespoons grated gruyère *or* cheddar cheese
1 cup fromage frais *or* natural yogurt
3 tablespoons wholemeal breadcrumbs

Preheat the oven to gas mark 6, 400°F (200°C). Peel the turnips and cut into small chunks. Blanch in boiling slightly salted water for 5 minutes. Drain. Heat the butter in a heavy pan and fry the garlic for 2 minutes. Add the turnip pieces and fry together for 2 minutes. Turn into a greased ovenproof dish. Season with salt and pepper and sprinkle over the herbs. Cover with the cheese and pour over the fromage frais, spreading to cover as necessary. Cover with the breadcrumbs and bake in the oven until the top is crisp and golden (about 30 minutes).

Turnips with Herbs
(*Navets aux Fines Herbes*)

Serves 4

1½ lb (675 g) turnips
salt
3 tablespoons melted butter
freshly ground black pepper
1 teaspoon chopped sage
1 teaspoon chopped chives
1 teaspoon chopped tarragon
1 teaspoon chopped thyme *or* parsley
4-inch (10-cm) piece cucumber, sliced
2 tomatoes, sliced

Peel the turnips and cut into chunks. Boil in slightly salted water until just tender. Slice the turnip chunks. Heat the butter in a heavy pan over a low heat. Add the turnip slices and season well with pepper. Turn in the butter for 3 minutes. Add the herbs and turn for 1 minute. Put onto a serving dish and garnish with cucumber and tomato slices.

Glazed Turnips (*Navets Glacés*)

Serves 4

2 lb (900 g) small turnips
salt
3 tablespoons butter
1 cup stock
1 tablespoon caster *or* icing sugar
freshly ground black pepper

Peel the turnips and cut into small pieces. Cook in a pan of boiling slightly salted water for 15 minutes. Drain. Put the butter in a heavy pan and melt over a low heat. Add the turnips, stock and sugar and pepper to taste. Allow to cook over a gentle heat until all the liquid has evaporated and the turnips are coated in a thick syrup.

Glossary

ail	garlic
artichaut	artichoke
asperge	asparagus
basilic	basil
beignet	fritter
bette	Swiss chard
betterave	beetroot
beurre	butter
blea	Swiss chard (Provence)
bourbonnais	Bourbon
braisé	braised
en branche	whole stalks
brouillé	scrambled (of eggs)
carotte	carrot
à la catalane	in the style of Catalonia
céleri	celery
céleri-rave	celeriac
cerfeuil	chervil
champignon	mushroom
chèvre	goat
chou	cabbage
chou-fleur	cauliflower
chou rouge	red cabbage
choux de Bruxelles	Brussels sprouts
ciboule	spring onion, scallion
concombre	cucumber
courge	marrow
à la crème	with cream or cream sauce
crêpe	pancake
cresson	watercress
croquette	croquette, patty
épinards	spinach

endive	chicory
farci	stuffed
fenouil	fennel
fermière	farmer's wife
feuille	leaf
fève	broad bean
fines herbes	culinary herbs
au four	baked (in the oven)
fromage	cheese
galette	pancake, crêpe, cake
gâteau	cake
glacé	glazed, chilled, frozen
gratin	baked dish, topped with cheese or breadcrumbs
haricot	haricot (white) bean
haricot verts	French (green) beans
jeudi	Thursday
laitue	lettuce
légume	vegetable
à la liégeoise	in the style of Liège, Belgium
maïs	sweetcorn
marron	chestnut
menthe	mint
Midi	south of France
navet	turnip
noix	walnut
oeuf	egg
oignon	onion
oseille	sorrel
pain	bread
panais	parsnip
pâté	pie, cake, patty
paysanne	country woman
petits pois	small peas
pissenlit	dandelion (literally 'piss in bed')
pistou	paste made from basil, garlic and parmesan cheese
poché	poached
pois	pea
pois chiche	chick pea
poireau	leek
poivron	green or red sweet pepper

polonais	Polish
pomme	apple
pomme de terre	potato
potage	soup
potiron	pumpkin
quiche	flan
ragoût	stew
riz	rice
salade	salad, lettuce
tomate	tomato
tourte	pie (Provence)
velouté	velvety, creamy (as of a white sauce)
vendanges	grape harvest
vert	green
vinaigrette	sauce or dressing made with wine vinegar and olive oil and seasoned